John D. Sutherland
1976

B. C.

−lc

THE PATRISTIC DOCTRINE
OF REDEMPTION

THE
PATRISTIC DOCTRINE
OF REDEMPTION

*A Study of the Development of Doctrine
during the First Five Centuries*

BY

H. E. W. TURNER

*Sometime Fellow of Lincoln College, Oxford; Canon of Durham;
and Lightfoot Professor of Divinity in the University of Durham*

LONDON
A. R. MOWBRAY & Co. LIMITED
NEW YORK : MOREHOUSE-GORHAM CO.

First published in 1952

PRINTED IN GREAT BRITAIN BY
A. R. MOWBRAY & CO. LIMITED IN THE CITY OF OXFORD
2998

TO MY MOTHER
IN AFFECTION AND GRATITUDE

PREFACE

THIS work is based upon a series of lectures which were given at *Scholae Cancellariae*, Lincoln, during Passion Week, 1949, on the invitation of the Warden, the Reverend Canon C. K. Sansbury. It is a laudable custom of the College during Passion Week each year to invite an outside lecturer to lecture upon some subject connected with the Passion of our Lord.

The doctrine of Redemption among the early Fathers has never received the attention by scholars which it deserves. The reasons for this neglect are many and various. Scholars primarily concerned with the doctrine of the Atonement normally tend to hurry over the early centuries and to begin a serious discussion with the teaching of S. Anselm and of Peter Abelard, at whose hands the doctrine first begins to take a definite shape. Others select from the patristic material the passages and allusions which fit best into their own preferred doctrinal mould, without paying adequate attention to complementary patterns of thought which possess equal significance. Others again, because of the number and complexity of the issues involved, tend to leave the subject on one side, on the ground that the thinking of the Fathers is not sufficiently clear-cut and precise for anyone except the expert.

This little book is offered to the ordinary reader interested in Theology in the hope that it may convince him that the early Christian centuries did think honestly and interestingly about the central experience of their religion; to the theological student as a guide to a dark place; and to the expert as a reminder of a serious gap in theological bibliography and as a challenge to go into the land and possess it.

My thanks are due to Mrs. Susan Fish for the typing of the manuscript, in addition to many other duties cheerfully and ably undertaken.

H. E. W. TURNER

CONTENTS

THE PATRISTIC DOCTRINE
OF REDEMPTION

CHAPTER 1

INTRODUCTION

THERE is, perhaps, no really satisfactory treatment of
the doctrine of Redemption during the period of the
Early Fathers. Most writers on the subject of the
Death of Christ offer little more than a rather super-
ficial summary of the earlier period before passing on
to the more familiar period in which the forest-track
of patristic thinking is replaced by the metalled road
of Anselmic and post-Anselmic speculation on the
subject. In English the best treatment is still the
well-documented earlier lectures of Rashdall,[1] but
his conclusions, legitimate against those who believe
that the only doctrine of the Atonement which can
claim to be either true or Biblical is a substitutionary
view, stress unduly the inspiratory and illuminative
character of the Death of Christ. Yet it would be
rather surprising if either Abelard or S. Anselm
taken by himself represented the full truth about the
Patristic period. Nor was Dr. Rashdall ever well
adapted, either by temperament or by equipment, to
penetrate below the surface of views or expressions

---

[1] H. Rashdall, *The Idea of Atonement in Christian Theology.*

which appeared to him exaggerated or absurd. He was less interested in inquiring what the Fathers were really meaning than in deciding what statements of theirs were acceptable to the high ethical standards of his essential Liberalism. Here, as in all else that Dr. Rashdall wrote, we can be sure that Christianity means at least what he said that it meant; the trouble is that in certain respects it is probable that it means a great deal more besides. There is, however, no doubt that Peter Abelard, had he lived in the patristic period, would have found many ideas and passages which might lend some support to his views.

The best and most recent attempt to deal with this 'overplus' of significance in the patristic period has been made by G. Aulén, whose work, originally written in Swedish, has been translated by Father Hebert, under the title of *Christus Victor*. In essentials it is an attempt, as brilliant as it is sympathetic, to penetrate beneath the surface of the symbolism of the defeat of the demons which plays so much part in the doctrine of Redemption in the patristic period, and which Dr. Rashdall virtually leaves on one side. Although, however, Dr. Aulén offers an illuminating contrast between the *Christus Victor* and the 'Christ Victim' views of which I have made full use, he does not attempt either to review the passages on which Dr. Rashdall relied or to analyse other views, particularly in the Greek Fathers, which bear upon the doctrine without using the symbolism with which he is chiefly concerned.

Of Continental works, I have used in the main

the standard Histories of Dogma by Loofs, Harnack, and Seeberg[1] and the more recent work by Dr. Martin Werner of Berne University: brilliant, exhaustive, well-documented, and perverse.[2] In French there is the careful study of Rivière[3] and a few well arranged pages in the *Histoire* of J. Turmel,[4] which belongs to the period of the extreme French Modernism.

The chief problem of any treatment of the doctrine of Redemption in the patristic period is one of acclimatization. We are concerned with the formative period of Christian thought, and it would be idle to proceed to it with the preconceptions derived from later controversies and their assumptions. The Church had at best the religious tradition of the New Testament and the Apostolic Church to guide its thought. Its experience of Redemption through Christ was far richer than its attempted formulations of this experience. The *lex orandi* was here, as always, prior to the *lex credendi*. It possessed the *Heilsgeschichte*, the focal points of the historical Redemption wrought by God through Christ, mediated through the Spirit and actualized within the Fellowship. The epochal moments of New Testament revelation were fixed points. These were embodied first in the *Kerugma*,[5] the proclamation of these saving facts, and at a slightly later stage, the Creed[6] considered as a

---

[1] F. Loofs, *Leitfaden zum Studien der Dogmengeschichte*; A. Harnack, *Lehrbuch der Dogmengeschichte*; R. Seeberg, *Lehrbuch der Dogmengeschichte*.
[2] M. Werner, *Die Entstehung des Christlichen Dogmas*.
[3] J. Rivière, *Le dogme de la Redemption*.
[4] J. Turmel, *Histoire des Dogmes*, Vol. i, pp. 352–80.
[5] C. H. Dodd, *The Apostolic Preaching and its Development*.
[6] J. de Ghellinck, *Patristique et Moyen Age*, Vol. i; J. N. D. Kelly, *Early Christian Creeds*.

catalogue of subjects of belief, used first for catechetical and baptismal purposes with the minimum of
doctrinal expansion until the Arian and subsequent
controversies made it imperative to proceed to further
doctrinal definition in order to exclude false teaching.
Even here, though many of these views had far-
reaching implications for the doctrine of Redemption,
the subject of Redemption itself is little more than
incidentally included. In addition to the Creed there
seems to have been the 'Rule of Faith,' more prominent
in the West than in the East, based upon, though not
identical with, the Creed. A detailed study of the
Regula Fidei is one of the more urgent needs of
patristic scholarship at the present time.

It will readily be seen that besides these fixed
elements in the Christian tradition, there were many
elements in which flexibility and variation had their
full part to play. These variable elements were given
full scope in the construction of patristic theology,
and consist first, in the intellectual categories in which
theology was framed; secondly, in the individual
emphasis of particular theologians; and thirdly, in
the common characteristics of schools of theologians
associated with the great sees and schools of Christian
theology in the early centuries.

The motives which led the Church to express her
lex orandi in intellectual and theological form fall
roughly into two classes. The religious realities in
which she lived needed to be formulated defensively
against rival systems without Christianity as well as
within. Christianity was not produced against a

tabula rasa. It was only one of many competing religious and philosophical systems, and though certain factors favoured its growth and expansion, its intervention in the early centuries could only be successful if it came to grips with other factors less favourable to its growth. Whereas in the sphere of religion the emphasis upon saving historical facts gave it an attraction which no other competitor for the soul of the world could possess, there was much need for it to come to terms with the massive intellectual construction of Greek philosophy upon which, by this time, much of the religion of the Græco-Roman world had come to base itself. The problem of 'communication' needed to be honestly faced if Christianity were not to become simply a 'warm' emotional cult, similar in effect, if not in structure and material, to the Eastern Mystery Religions, competing for the satisfaction of the religious needs of the world, and the Church more than a home of like-minded pietists without any fruitful means of impingement upon the intellectual as well as the emotional thought-climate of contemporary society.

This 'apologetic' aspect of theology had certain fundamental questions which were forced upon its attention by the 'missionary' situation of early Christianity. How could Christians indulge in their normal polemic against polytheism if at the heart of their Gospel lay the insistence upon the full Divinity of our Lord? They claimed to be the heirs of Jewish Monotheism and the fulfilment *malgré lui* of pagan philosophical monism. Clearly the vindication of

B

the full Deity of our Lord which lay at the heart of their *lex orandi* was first charge upon their intellectual resources. Only less urgent was the duty of expounding their teaching about the Person of the Incarnate Lord Himself, and the reconciliation of the Divine and human elements which met in Him. On the apologetic side the Church seems almost to have worked to an agenda: the Unity of the Godhead, finally formulated at the Council of Nicaea; the status of the three co-equal entities within the Godhead, which reached doctrinal maturity by the time of the Council of Constantinople; and the problem of the Person of Christ, which received credal expression at the Council of Chalcedon.

Now it is not to be thought that any Christian thinker merely confined himself to the primary subject of the Church's apologetic task at his particular epoch. Christian theology is not merely 'Christianity defensively stated.' It is also entrusted with the duty of 'Christian self-expression.' The *lex orandi* itself on the religious level is composed of a number of factors, each of which is interrelated to the others and which can only be lived as a total system of prayer and devotion. This need to integrate and to evaluate the various elements in the Christian *lex orandi* might well have been the primary motive in the formation of Christian orthodoxy. It would certainly have been so if the Church had not to a considerable extent been compelled to produce its theology 'under fire.' It is wholly typical of the state of affairs that the most important works of Christian theology up to the time of Origen's *De Principiis* take the form of treatises directed to the pagan, Jewish, or heretical opponents of the Church. The principal problems for theological consideration were not necessarily those which stood closest to the heart of the *lex orandi* as such, but those which offered the most important bridgeheads into paganism or which gave the greatest difficulty to pagans who wished to make contact with Christianity.

This is not to say, of course, that by a kind of theological Self-denying Ordinance, the Christian theologians of the early centuries confined their attention to matters which were of direct apologetic concern, but rather that we can be sure that they gave the forefront of their attention to the problems which were of greatest relevance to their own day.

Two examples will serve to make this plain. S. Athanasius is above all the Doctor of the Holy Trinity. In his arguments against the Arians and in defence of the Nicene faith, he moves with a certain assurance of step and firmness of touch. Yet he clearly could not avoid handling both the doctrines of the Person of Christ and of Redemption as one who lived richly within the whole Christian *lex orandi*. Certainly his treatment of the Doctrine of the Person of Christ does not possess quite the same assurance as his formulation of the doctrine of the Trinity, and while there is much in his doctrine of Redemption which is wisely and rightly said, the same fundamental criticism can be made here as well. Again, the Cappadocian Fathers, at their best in the treatment of the doctrine of the Holy Spirit and of the Three Hypostases of the

Holy Trinity, are not equally successful in the less immediately pressing problems of the doctrines of the Person of Christ, Redemption, and of Sacramental Grace.

If, then, the apologetic motive were the primary one which led to the evolution of Christian theology during this period, it can be readily understood why the doctrine of Redemption would arise for systematic clarification later rather than sooner. If the primary principles of the Christian faith were in grave need of defence and justification from the point of view of pagan inquirers, the theological corollaries dependent upon these axioms would need to be left to a later stage in the debate. While no doubt many pagan souls were finding Redemption through Christ a living fact in their experience, the general impression left by the Christian experience of Redemption upon the thoughtful pagan, as revealed in the fragments of the *Alethes Logos* of Celsus and elsewhere, was little short of bewilderment. Until the Christian idea of God and his valuation of Christ could be put into their correct proportion, Redemption, as the Christian understood it, won, and mediated through Christ, would remain as a kind of religious 'surd.' If the *via crucis* were all the time being followed religiously, the *theologia crucis* lagged somewhat until other elements in Christian Theology were set in a clearer light.

While, then, the question *Cur Deus Homo?* was raised at times during the period under review, and notably by S. Irenaeus and S. Athanasius, the conditions for a full-scale answer were hardly, as yet, present. A second feature which militated against the evolution of a closely knit and highly developed doctrine of Redemption during the early centuries lies in the large number of 'concomitant variables' involved in any statement of the doctrine. Some of these factors involved problems to which the secular thought of the day offered no agreed answer; others, more specifically belonging to the Jewish and Christian tradition, were matters of speculation capable of several different types of phrasing. An example of the first type of factor is the problem, 'What constitutes a human being?' The problem of psychology, to which at least two main types of solution were being offered in contemporary Greek thinking, is inevitably involved both in the nature of the God-Man and in the effect upon man of the Redemption which He brought. Again the problem, peculiar to Judaism and Christianity, of what man lost through the Fall and what was restored to him in Redemption, was capable of different forms of expression during the period with which we are concerned. Traditions which emphasized the mediation of Redemption through the Sacramental Life raised the further question of the nature and effect of the Christian Sacraments.

Examples of the influence of these problems upon the doctrine of Redemption during the formative period are not hard to find. Theories which see in Redemption the restoration of incorruption and immortality receive physical, metaphysical, and mystical treatment in the light of what individual Fathers considered to have been lost by the Fall. Even more significant is the influence of the doctrine of the Person of Christ upon the doctrine of Redemption. Is Redemption seen primarily as the act of the incarnate Lord or as the rescue effected by the Logos Himself? Besides the *Christus Victor* theory which forms a dominant theme in the earlier centuries can be traced a *Logos Victor* theory. In the first the Humanity of the Incarnate Lord is considered as the very element in and through which His Vicarious Victory was achieved for us men and for our salvation. In the second type of theory the Humanity of our Lord is considered rather as the base of operations against the demonic powers, or at worst as the bait used to catch the devil while the Divine *Logos* played the line. The decline and transmutation of the older primitive eschatology again affects the terms and the concepts under which the doctrine of Redemption can be plausibly stated.

A third element of fluidity in early formulations of the doctrine of Redemption is involved in the fact that particularly in the East the decisive moment in the incarnate life of our Lord is never adequately pin-pointed. Western Christians naturally tend to see in the Death and Passion of our Lord the events in which our Redemption is focused. This is not indeed over-looked in the early centuries, but such a view if pressed too hard has always found it difficult to explain how Christ could forgive sins during His earthly life. The whole Incarnation is seen by the Fathers as involved in the decisive act of our Redemption. This depends not merely upon the dying Christ, nor upon the dying and rising Christ, but upon the Total Christ. It might well have been expected that

the *Christus Victor* theory at least would find it
necessary to offer a more careful analysis of the focal
moment of Redemption, but we shall find reason to
believe that even here more emphasis is laid upon the
effects of Redemption rather than the precise moment
of its accomplishment. Many early Fathers would
have found little difficulty in accepting the gently
satirical adaptation of Mrs. Alexander's well-known
hymn, offered by Bishop Kirk[1] in the interests of some
exemplarist theories:

> He lived that we might be forgiven,
> He lived to make us good,
> That we might go at last to Heaven
> Saved by His previous love.

Only they would have found as little difficulty with
the authentic version! The medieval and modern
tendency to set Incarnation and Atonement in opposi-
tion would have had little meaning for them.

A further element of flexibility is introduced by
the very conditions of the fact of Redemption itself,
though here the patristic period is under no special
disadvantage as compared with later formulations.
It appears to be inherent to Christianity that its
structure should appear to be paradoxical—an ultimate
monism supporting, and supported by, a temporary
dualism. Christianity involves the paradox of a life-
and-death struggle of which the ultimate issue is never
for one moment in doubt. Every doctrine of Redemption, at one stage or another of its development, is

---

[1] K. E. Kirk, 'The Atonement,' in *Essays Catholic and Critical*, p. 250.
It should, of course, be said that Dr. Kirk himself by no means holds such
a view.

faced with this problem and few more decisively than the *Christus Victor* theory. Turmel[1] indeed sees this dualism as a loan from Marcionism in which the good and evil gods of this system are taken over as God and the Devil into orthodox Christianity, and played off the one against the other. This depends in part upon the late second-century dating of the New Testament documents which he maintains, and in which he has found few reputable scholars to follow him. The data of Jewish eschatology and the more probable dates of the New Testament writings support rather a reversal of his hypothesis, that Marcionism represents a bowdlerization and coarsening of the data more correctly interpreted by Christian Orthodoxy. Aulén is certainly right in talking of a certain relative dualism as endemic to Christianity itself.[2]

Again, there is a curious two-sidedness about the Christian doctrine of Redemption to which even more prominently attention is drawn by Aulén.[3] Redemption is not only an act wrought by God on our behalf; there is also a sense in which something is here offered to God in the Humanity of Christ. Besides the *Christus Victor* theory in the early Fathers there stands the Christ Victim theory, and both often lie side by side in the same author, particularly in the West. The *Christus Victor* theory stresses what was wrought through Christ by God on behalf of man; the Christ Victim theory emphasizes what was offered as man by Christ for men before God. The action, as

---

[1] J. Turmel, *Histoire des Dogmes*, i, pp. 329–32.
[2] *Christus Victor*, p. 20, n. 1.   [3] ibid., pp. 12–16.

it were, takes place on two simultaneous planes. Later theories by their preoccupation with one tend to under-emphasize the other. In more modern parlance the so-called subjective theories represent an attenuated form of the first; the objective theories a partial and limited phrasing of the second. These features naturally militate against any complex formulation of the doctrine during the formative period of Christian orthodoxy.

This may serve as an attempted introduction to the patristic period in general, what we may be entitled to expect from it by way of formulation, and the principal obstacles to a more coherent expression of the doctrine which we are to study. We must be content to find the Fathers thinking along more traditional or conventional lines here than is the case with other doctrines of greater or more immediate concern. Nor shall we find the background issues at all fully explored. Yet to contrast them too sharply with a S. Anselm or a Peter Abelard is to do little justice to the task which they were undertaking or to the essential character of the formulations towards which they were feeling their way.

That we are not in error in making this distinction between the doctrine of Redemption during the patristic period and that which later came to fruition within the Church can be proved by three significant points:

(a) Dr. Rashdall points out with perfect truth that in the earliest period the Fathers seem to be content to appeal to the Scriptural basis for the doctrine,

whether in the New Testament records or in Old
Testament prophecy. This is no doubt what we should
expect with writers whose surviving treatises are
so largely and directly based upon the Bible in
commentary or homily. But it has an additional
significance as confirmatory evidence that we are
here nearer to the Biblical 'law of prayer' than to the
formulations of a philosophically orientated theology.

(*b*) One of the most interesting features of the
patristic period is the steady retreat from anything
which could be described as authentic Paulinism.
This has been recently noted (with undue exaggeration
of the amount of such 'Paulinism' within the New
Testament itself) by Dr. T. F. Torrance.[1] Despite such
defences as those by Werner[2] and more recently by
Mr. F. H. Lawson[3] with regard to S. Irenaeus, it still
remains true that the monumental genius of S. Paul
had little permanent influence on the theology of the
early Church. His writings are used rather as a quarry
for proof-texts than as a coherent system accepted as
a whole. All the more striking, therefore, is the fact
that the Pauline image of Redemption as victory over
the demons is retained as a dominant theme by many
Fathers during the whole patristic period. Indeed,
Celsus seems to imply that this is almost the official
doctrine of the Church on the subject.[4] Now it is
certainly true that belief in demons is still incorporated
in the *lex orandi* of the Church in the early centuries.

---

[1] *Grace in the Apostolic Fathers.*   [2] *Der Paulinismus des Irenaeus.*
[3] *The Biblical Theology of S. Irenaeus.*
[4] Celsus in Origen, *c. Cels.* ii. 47, vi. 42.

Celsus and his later opponent, Origen, were at one in believing that they existed; what divided them was the question of the right and proper attitude towards them for mankind to adopt. Paulinism, already in retreat so far as its distinctive doctrines were concerned, still retains its grip in this respect upon the phrasing of the Church's beliefs on Redemption.

(c) Eschatology is still a vexed question among New Testament scholars, but whether with Turmel[1] we speak of the transmutation of an older nationalist eschatology or with Werner[2] of the Church's theology as a substitute for older eschatology, or whether, as is more likely, quite another phrasing of this fact will be ultimately preferred by scholars, it still remains true that the period with which we are concerned marks a steady decline in the interest of the early Church in eschatology. The fortunes of the doctrine called *chiliasm* (the belief in the reign of our Lord with His saints for a thousand years upon the earth) might serve as a kind of barometer of the fortunes of eschatology. But it is precisely in regard to the doctrine of Redemption that eschatology remains the longest in its primitive form. Werner, who suspects the evolution of Christian theology as a kind of illicit surrogate for the earlier eschatology, himself affords the evidence which suggests that eschatology retained its grip on the doctrine of Redemption longer and more vitally than in many other branches of patristic theology.

---

[1] *Histoire des Dogmes*, vol. i, pp. 320-5.
[2] M. Werner, *Die Entstehung des Christlichen Dogmas*, pp. 289-301.

Such facts, then, put beyond doubt the fact that the doctrine of Redemption remained at the 'expressional' level longer than most other doctrines, and that the expectation which we have been led to form that we should be likely to find ourselves furthest from scientific formulation and nearest to the religious realities of the *lex orandi* is not illusory.

There have been many attempts to analyse the doctrine in the patristic period. Rashdall has proved that the concept of the death of Christ as an example is not foreign to the thought of the Fathers, though there is much in the evidence which he fails to interpret with sympathy and imagination. Aulén, piercing below the surface of the superficially unattractive imagery used by many of the Fathers, has successfully rescued from oblivion the *Christus Victor* theory which he sets side by side with the Christ Victim view. More elaborate classifications are offered by Rivière who divides the material into juridical, political, and poetical views.[1] The first of his subdivisions is largely the Christ Victim theory, the third the *Christus Victor* view, while the second really cuts across the other two suggested classifications. H. Mandel[2] distinguishes an earlier cosmological-ontological view from a later ethical-religious. Quite apart from the criticism that this evolution reverses all the laws of development which a historian of dogma would expect, it must be noted that the ethical

---

[1] J. Rivière, *Le Dogme de la Redemption.*
[2] Quoted by G. Aulén, *Christus Victor*, p. 53.

and religious valuation of the Redemptive work of
Christ persists throughout the period. While it might
be said that the cosmological significance of the
Redemption wrought by Christ interpreted in terms of
eschatology and *Christus Victor* thinking is early,
the ontological implications of Redemption do not
come to the fore until the time of Origen. Werner
distinguishes an early cosmological-eschatological
view which in part continues throughout the period,
though its eschatological assumptions and implications are left hanging in the air, from a later metaphysical and sacramental view.[1] He is largely right in
one half of each of his pairs of adjectives. The earlier
views are more eschatologically phrased than the later,
while the later views are much more aware of the
metaphysical implications of the doctrine than the
earlier. While the Cappadocians and other later
thinkers lay great stress upon the sacramental mediation of the death of Christ, such associations cluster
round it as early as S. Ignatius' description of the
Eucharist as 'the medicine of immortality.' Again, it
would certainly be hard to discuss the doctrine of
Redemption in S. Athanasius without becoming aware
of the cosmological significance which he attaches to
it. Turmel is surprisingly more satisfactory in the
classifications which he proposes for the subject '*Le
Christ Docteur, le Christ principe de vie divine, le Christ
victime expiatoire,*' with an appendix upon the doctrine
of '*le Rachat au Diable*' which in part overlaps what

[1] M. Werner, *Die Entstehung des Christlichen Dogmas*, pp. 271–89.

Aulén would call the *Christus Victor* theory.[1] It may be appropriate to take as our suggested classification here four heads: Christ the Illuminator, Christ the Victor, Christ the Giver of Incorruption and Deification, and Christ the Victim.

[1] J. Turmel, *Histoire des Dogmes*, vol. i, pp. 333-45.

CHAPTER II

CHRIST THE ILLUMINATOR

THE description of the death of Christ as an example, with the ideas related to it, certainly occurs sporadically in the New Testament itself. The theme 'as is the Master, so shall the servant be' underlies the teaching of Jesus Himself in the Gospels. That the death of Christ is an example is expressly stated in the First Epistle of S. Peter, where the practical aim of the author made this aspect of the Atonement especially significant.[1] Even the famous hymn to the Humiliated and Exalted Christ, so often quoted as evidence for S. Paul's Christology, is introduced for a practical purpose. 'Let this mind be in you which was also in Christ Jesus.'[2]

Two facts suggest that this aspect of the death of Christ was not likely to be foreign to the thought of the patristic period.

I. There is a group of passages which stress the parallel between the death of Christ and the self-sacrifice of others, pagans as well as Christians. S. Ignatius can describe himself as a substitute for his fellow-Christians.[3] That this is no personal idiosyncrasy, born of the teeming brain of the martyr-bishop of Antioch, is proved by the fact that the same theory underlies the claim of the confessors, 'the spoilt

[1] 1 Pet. ii. 21. [2] Phil. ii. 5–11. [3] Ignatius, *Eph.* xxi. 1, ἀντίψυχον

children of the Early Church,' during the periods of general persecution to act almost as an alternative channel of reconciliation beside the developing penitential system. Their suffering for Christ, like His for them, could avail to atone for sin. Origen finds no cause for quarrel with the contention of Celsus that acts of self-sacrifice are well known in pagan religions.[1] That this is no mere admission wrung from him in the heat of debate is proved by the fact that he later returns to the same theme in the Commentary on S. John.[2] 'Pagan records offer no contemptible parallels to the death of Christ' and 'Akin to His sacrifice are the rest, of which the symbols are those of the Law' and 'Other related sacrifices appear to me to be the outpourings of the blood of noble martyrs.'[3] Such an idea could not fail to be congenial to one whose own father had been a notable martyr.

Two things are worthy of note in this connexion. The significance of such passages is unquestionable. They imply that the sacrifice of Christ differs only in degree from that of other heroes. Such a view would be anathema to the 'objective' theory of the Atonement, especially those forms which tend to express the significance of the death of Christ in transactional language. Such a difference in degree is fundamentally irreconcilable with the 'once-for-allness' which this view demands. Yet, as against Harnack and Werner, it must be admitted that at least in the case of Origen, such passages represent only one element in a many-sided view of the Redemption wrought through Christ.

[1] Origen, *c. Cels*. i. 31. [2] ibid., *Comm. in Jo.*, xxviii. 19. [3] ibid., vi. 54.

They must be held in solution with other insights and significances.

II. Other passages make much of the argument from prophecy in connexion with the death of Christ. In theory, no doubt, this might be acceptable even to the most thorough-going of objective views, but during this period they fit more naturally into the framework of the death of Christ considered as a demonstration of the Redemptive purpose of God towards mankind revealed in a particular set of mighty works. The argument is not, of course, confined to the earlier period of Christian thought, but it has a special significance then in view of the absence of more clear-cut views. It may mean as little theologically as a mere repetition without further theologizing of the primitive Christian *lex orandi*, 'that Christ died for our sins according to the Scriptures,'[1] but it possesses in many cases a far deeper significance, a genuine theological attempt to fit the death of Christ into a total argument from the Mighty Acts of God. The argument from miracle, the other main form of this approach to pagans, was less decisive. Jesus Himself never claims to be the only wonder-worker.[2] Miracle was claimed even by pagans themselves, the Temple of Aesculapius at Delos proving a veritable pagan Lourdes. Celsus is quick to point out the existence even of 'greater works than these' in the form of pagan parallels to the miracles of our Lord, and

[1] i Cor. xv. 3.
[2] Matthew xii. 27, Luke xi. 19. 'If I by Beelzebub cast out devils, by whom do your sons cast them out?'

Origen is not prepared to dispute the matter with him.[1] The argument from prophecy had, however, greater significance for Christian apologetic. The pagan world, on the whole, believed devoutly in oracles,[2] though their achievements fell far short of what Christians claimed as the organic relation between the Old Testament prophecies and the New Testament fulfilments. As used against the Jews, though here it needed defence and argument in support, its effect was little short of devastating. Its significance has, however, been somewhat obscured in a period when Biblical theology has been wellnigh replaced by Biblical criticism. The *Dialogue* of S. Justin against Trypho turns largely on this argument. One passage alone may be quoted by way of illustration.[3] 'If this fact (suffering and death according to the Scriptures) characterizes Him and points Him out to all, how could we also have failed with confidence to believe in Him?' Isaiah liii is the natural proof-text,[4] but a typological interpretation of the Old Testament is also adduced as a supporting argument. The sacrifice of Isaac,[5] the brazen serpent,[6] the outstretched hands of Moses,[7] are all used as types, while for the connexion between the death on the Cross and Holy

[1] Origen, *c. Cels.* v. 57.
[2] For the pagan belief in oracles see F. W. H. Myers, *Essays Classical,* and for one theory (Plutarch's) of oracular inspiration see G. Verbeke, *L'Evolution de la Doctrine du Pneuma,* pp. 267–86.
[3] Justin, *Dial.* 89.
[4] ibid., *Apo.* i. 50–1. Asiatic Elders (Routh, *Reliquiae Sacrae* i, p. 56). *I Clement,* 16.
[5] *Barnabas,* vii. 3.   [6] ibid., xii. 5–7.
[7] *Barnabas,* xii. 2; Justin, *Dial.* 131.

Baptism, Jeremiah and Ezekiel afford somewhat surprising Old Testament warrant.[1]

Straightforward appeals to the Passion in moral exhortations are frequently found. *I Clement*[2] echoes the Kenotic passage in Philippians without, however, any trace of the rich theology so typical of the Pauline passage. 'For if the Lord were so humble-minded, what should we do who came through Him under the yoke of His grace?' S. Polycarp again in his letter to the Philippians[3] comments as follows on Isaiah liii: 'But He endured all this that we might live. Let us therefore become imitators of His endurance and, if we suffer for His Name, let us glorify Him. For He made this an example to us and we believed it.' Later writers combine this strain of thinking about the Passion with other elements more characteristic of their thought. S. Irenaeus says: 'The Word is our Master and we must be imitators of His works and doers of His words'[4]; while on Romans iv. 7 Origen comments: 'Jesus Christ justifies solely those who take up a new life through the example of the Resurrection and cast aside the old garment of injustice and iniquity as a case of death.'[5]

The interpretation of the Redemption which Christ brought primarily in terms of knowledge, and of Christ first and foremost a Teacher, is especially characteristic of the Apostolic Fathers. The Eucharistic prayer in the *Didache* twice offers thanks for the knowledge, life,

---

[1] *Barnabas*, xi. 1–2, 8, 11, quoting Jeremiah ii. 13, Ezekiel xlvii. 1–12.
[2] *I Clement*, 16.   [3] Polycarp, *Phil.* viii. 1–2.
[4] Irenaeus, *Adv. Haer. Omn.* v. 1, 1 (Harvey ii, p. 314).
[5] Origen, *In Rom.* iv. 7.

faith, and immortality brought through the Servant-Son Jesus.[1] The *Shepherd* of Hermas contains a curious parable which speaks of the Servant made co-heir with the Son for services rendered in the vineyard, and the interpretation appended to it makes it clear that the work of supererogation is to be identified with the teaching office of our Lord.[2] 'Having Himself thus cleansed the sins of the people, He showed them the paths of life, giving to them the Law which He received from His Father.' It is, of course, possible that under the figure of a hendiadys Hermas is including both the redemptive work and the teaching office of Christ under this head. Certainly neither the style nor the theology of Hermas can be deemed to be above reproach. There is a similar, though not quite so clear-cut passage in the anonymous *Epistle to Diognetus* which describes His coming to man, as saving, using persuasion not force (for force is no attribute of God), calling not persecuting, loving not judging.[3] While, no doubt, this element is integral to any picture of the theology of Redemption through Christ, it would prove particularly congenial to the highly moralistic, relatively undogmatic, theology which was so dominant a feature of early second-century Christianity.

It recurs freely among the later and more practical-minded Western theologians. It is especially characteristic of writers like Lactantius and Arnobius, philosophers converted late in life, whose theology never wholly embodies the fulness of the Christian tradition. A typical passage may be quoted from

[1] *Didache*, ix. 3, x. 2.   [2] Hermas, *Sim.* v. 6. 2–3.   [3] *Epist. ad Diog.* vii. 4.

Lactantius as an example. 'It is necessary that one who undertakes to teach virtue should be like men, so that by overcoming sin, He could show by example that sin could be overcome.' To the charge 'You are asking impossibilities,' He could reply, 'It is not impossible because I do it Myself.' He further interprets the healing of the leper as the type of the beneficent action of doctrine upon the souls which it purifies from sin.[1]

If it be urged that Lactantius was a case of arrested doctrinal development, the evidence of S. Augustine in his earliest period as a Christian may well be quoted. In a very early work, written while he was still under the influence of Neoplatonism, S. Augustine can describe the whole life of the Son of God as a moral instruction,[2] while a letter, written at broadly the same period, assigns as the sole reason for the Incarnation the need to supply men with precepts and examples of virtue.[3] Neither passage represents the full richness of the thought of S. Augustine on the subject of Redemption. If this is where he started, it is certainly not where he ended. At least he did not need to un-learn this lesson in later days, but only to build upon it.

Besides the teaching and example of Christ we can set the concept of Christ as the source of Illumination. This can be well illustrated by a passage from the *Clementine Homilies* which had a wide currency as 'Sunday afternoon reading' in the early Church:

[1] Lactantius, *Div. Inst.* iv. 24. 16.
[2] Augustine, *De ver. relig.* xvi. 32, '*Tota itaque vita eius per hominem quem suscipere dignatus est, disciplina morum fuit.*'
[3] ibid., *Epist.* xi. 4.

'Christ gave light and saved His children, our spirit was blinded and we adored stone, wood, gold, silver, and metals. Thanks to Him the circle of darkness which shrouded us has been broken and we have recovered our sight.'[1] The same theme is frequent in the even earlier *First Epistle of Clement*: 'Through Him our spirit which is without intelligence and filled with obscurity spreads into the light.' 'Through Him the Master [God] has willed to make us taste the immortal knowledge.'[2] 'Through Jesus Christ God has called us from darkness to light, from ignorance to the knowledge of His glorious Name. Thou hast opened the eyes of our heart that they may know Thee.'[3] The quasi-liturgical, almost lyrical nature of these last two passages is not surprising in view of the use of the term 'illumination' as a semi-technical term for Baptism in the early centuries.

So far the passages to which attention has been called focus the saving teaching, example, and illumination upon the Historic Jesus. During the second century, however, the emphasis seems to shift from the Historic Jesus to the Divine *Logos*. Between the Apostolic Fathers and Clement of Alexandria we seem almost to cross a Christological watershed which affects here and elsewhere the whole phrasing of the doctrine of Redemption.

It was one of the abiding contributions of Professor F. Loofs of Halle to mark a clear distinction between two different concepts of the term *Logos* in the second

---

[1] *Clementine Homilies*, i. 4, quoted by Turmel, *Histoire des Dogmes*, i, p. 333.
[2] *I Clement*, xxxvi. 2.   [3] ibid., lix. 2.

century.[1] He pointed out a careful difference between
the significance of the term in the writings of such
Fathers as S. Ignatius, S. Irenaeus, and S. Theophilus
of Antioch, and those of the Apologists in general
and of Clement and Origen. It is proposed in these
chapters to mark the distinction by translating the
Greek term λόγος by Word when it is used in the
former sense and by offering the customary trans-
literation *Logos* in allusions to the latter tradition. The
Asiatic provenance of the Fathers who characterize the
former tradition led Loofs to maintain that it represents in the main an Asiatic speciality. Such a view
cannot, however, be substantiated fully, though it is
not without its attractions. It is, however, probable
that in the writings of these Fathers the Word is used
in a characteristic sense as the bearer of the Revelation
of God, through whom God speaks clearly to the
world, as it were with ringing tones so that all might
hear. The Cross of Christ is, for example, included
by S. Ignatius among the three mysteries of a loud cry
which were wrought in the silence of God.[2] The
Word proceeding from silence is Jesus Christ Who
reveals the One God.[3] For S. Irenaeus, too, the Word
is really God audible, 'the incomprehensible becoming
comprehensible, the invisible visible, the impassible
passible, and the Word Man.'[4] That with the revealing
function of the Word should be associated the teaching
office of Christ is what we might well expect. The
focus of this tradition which begins with the Word

[1] F. Loofs, *Paulus von Samosata*, p. 208; *Theophilus von Antiochien*, p. 248.
[2] Ignatius, *Eph.* 19. [3] ibid., *Magn.* viii. 2.
[4] Irenaeus, *Adv. Haer. Omn.* iii. 17. 6 (Harvey ii, p. 87); iv. 11. 4 (ii, p. 161).

is clearly carried over into the Incarnate Life of Christ. A typical passage in S. Irenaeus is the following: 'Not otherwise could we learn what God is if our Teacher the Word had not become Man. We could not otherwise learn unless we were to see our Teacher the Word and hear His voice with our ears, that we might become imitators of His actions and those who fulfil His words.'[1] On this passage Brunner comments rightly: 'Note how very clearly Irenaeus sees what it means to be the Word.'[2] This is what Loofs means when he speaks of the identity of Revelation between the Father and the Son as the hall-mark of this tradition. For the purpose of this particular emphasis the relation between Father and Son is drawn very close together—in fact, the closer the better if the Revelation vouchsafed through the Word is to have the full authority of the Father behind it.[3]

In the writings of the chief Apologists and the Alexandrine Fathers, Clement and Origen, the concept of the *Logos Revelator* occurs with a radically different thought-background. For S. Irenaeus the Word is God Himself revealing Himself in Christ;[4] for S. Justin He is another or a second God.[5] For S. Ignatius and S. Irenaeus the accent still falls upon the Historic and Incarnate Lord though it begins elsewhere; for the Apologists the emphasis lies rather upon the Dis-

---

[1] Irenaeus, *Adv. Haer. Omn.* v. 1. 1 (Harvey ii, p. 314).
[2] E. Brunner, *The Mediator*, p. 260.
[3] Loofs uses the term *Offenbarungsidentität* to express this relation. *Leitfaden*, p. 102; *Theophilus von Antiochien*, p. 355.
[4] Irenaeus, *Adv. Haer. Omn.* ii. 16. 4 (Harvey i, p. 285), '*Verbum est ipse Deus.*'
[5] Justin, *Dial.* 56 and 128.

carnate Lord. S. Irenaeus is deeply concerned with the Unity of the Father and the Son in revealing word and redeeming act; the Apologists focus their attention upon the *Logos* as a depotentiated God. S. Irenaeus concerns himself primarily with religion; the Apologists rather with philosophy. For them cosmology takes pride of place over soteriology, and Christianity is phrased rather as clear information about creation than as good news about redemption. S. Irenaeus stresses the uniqueness of the act of God in Christ; the Apologists prefer to dwell upon the Incarnation as a continuation of the work of the *Logos* before the coming of Christ. 'Those who before the coming of Christ lived in accordance with the Word were really Christians even though they were accounted atheists.'[1] 'Those who did the things which are universally, naturally and eternally good and well-pleasing to God will be saved through this same Jesus Christ in the resurrection no less than the just men who lived before them, Noah, Enoch, and Jacob and the rest who have recognized this Christ to be the Son of God.'[2] For S. Justin the Incarnation merely continues and exemplifies a process; it gives more of what is in some measure already available. Immanence and Incarnation differ not so much in kind as in degree. His answer to the question *Cur Deus Homo?* cannot be given in the same decisive tones as that of S. Irenaeus.

The thought of the Apologists is reiterated by Clement of Alexandria. He explicitly notes that all virtuous Jews and pagans will hereafter have the

[1] Justin, *Apol.* i. 46. [2] ibid., *Dial.* 45.

opportunity of entering the faith of Christ. He is the
first to bring 1 Peter iii. 18 f. into connexion with the
doctrine of the Descent into Hades, and probably
interprets it as evidence for the larger hope which he
accepts on general theological grounds.[1] Here we
find a proof-text, much in evidence in the *Christus
Victor* tradition, used to subserve the purpose of the
doctrine of Redemption as Illumination. Clement,
however, does make some attempt to distinguish
what the Greeks and others possessed through the
instrumentality of the *Logos* and what Christians enjoy
as a result of the Incarnation. The Greeks were indeed
justified through their philosophy, but the gift of
complete righteousness and perfect illumination came
through Jesus Christ. His emphasis, like that of the
Apologists, falls upon the Discarnate *Logos* and His
activity as the *Paidagogos* or Teacher of the human
race is central to his thought. Clement is a veritable
Apostle to the Greeks, a rôle well-suited to one who
sees in Greek philosophy a genuine preparation for
the Gospel.

But Clement has another rôle besides that of one of
the last of the Apologists and here, too, the concept
of Redemption as Illumination was bound to be laid
heavily under contribution. He is also one of the anti-
Gnostic Fathers and his defence of the Catholic Church
against Gnosticism bears the stamp of his own individual genius. Gnosticism sought to undercut the

[1] Clement Alex., *Strom.* vi. 6. 47. Loofs (s.v. Descent into Hades. *E.R.E.*
iv. 659b) notes that this interpretation of 1 Peter iii. 18 f. is followed by
Origen, *In Joann.* vi. 35. See also E. G. Selwyn, *The First Epistle of S. Peter*,
pp. 316 and 340.

success of Christianity by offering a little extra which ordinary Christianity did not appear to offer. For this the Gnostics might have claimed a slight, though genuine, New Testament authority. S. Paul, for example, spoke of a *Gnosis* which was the property of the perfect or mature Christian,[1] while the Second Epistle of S. Peter urged Christians to add to their faith knowledge.[2] Clement's attack upon *Gnosis* follows daring and individual lines. Whereas S. Irenaeus had been content to set the Christian and Gnostic *leges orandi* side by side with a certain amount of criticism of the content of the Gnostic pattern of belief, Clement seeks to turn the tables upon Gnosticism by showing that Christianity, rightly interpreted, could offer all that Gnosticism claimed to present. Celsus had referred in his usual terms of contempt to those Christians who made a tedious, and unenlightened appeal to faith and to faith alone.[3] Clement, on the other hand, sees the mature and enlightened Christian as the true Gnostic, a step ahead of the man of faith.[4] While the Gnostic systems make this distinction almost a matter of spiritual eugenics, treating the Gnostic or spiritual Christian as a race apart from the psychic or ordinary Catholic Christian, Clement normally regards the similar difference between the merely faithful and the 'knowledgeable' Christian as one of degree rather than of kind. Yet it must be admitted that at times he is led beyond the

[1] 1 Cor. ii. 6.   [2] 2 Pet. i. 5.   [3] Origen, *c. Cels.* i. 9.
[4] Clement Alex., *Strom.* vi. 14. 109 contrasts πιστεῦσαι and γνῶναι (see also O. Stählin, *Index in G.C.S.* vol. iv, s.v. πιστικὸς and γνωστικὸς for further examples of the contrast).

limits of his case as an orthodox Christian, as when he goes so far as to assign to the Christian Gnostic a different heaven from that enjoyed by the simple believer. The intellectual snobbery, endemic in Gnosticism, does not completely bye-pass the Christian answer given by Clement. His ideal Gnostic recalls the Stoic sage with his deep impassivity impervious to change and decay or any such thing. It is not surprising, therefore, to find in this part of his theology Redemption conceived as Illumination, Instruction, and Indoctrination. The Christian Gnostic is simply the Christian who has been led by the *Logos Paidagogos* beyond the faith on which his salvation rests to a Knowledge which lies strictly beyond faith.[1]

It is a far cry from the simple stress upon Jesus Christ the Teacher to the highly complex intellectualized picture of spiritual Illumination offered by Clement of Alexandria, with an eye less to the Gospels than to the defence of the Catholic Church alike against Greek philosophy and syncretistic Gnosticism. The root approach to the doctrine of Redemption has not, however, greatly changed, even though its form and character are vastly different.

A short analysis of the three groups of writers who belong most particularly to this tradition will help to set its significance in its true light.

---

[1] For the whole doctrine of Clement on the point see R. B. Tollinton, *Clement of Alexandria*, ch. 19; C. Bigg, *Christian Platonists of Alexandria*, pp. 123–32; and for the tensions which it set up in ecclesiastical circles, J. Lebreton, 'Le désaccord entre la foi populaire et la théologie savante,' *R.H.E.* xix, pp. 481–505, and xx, pp. 5–37. Lebreton notes the discreet silence of Origen on this whole concept.

I. *The Apostolic Fathers.* We can hardly overstress the importance in their writings of the idea of Christ the Teacher. Indeed, it appears to be their principal contribution to the doctrine of Redemption. This would appear natural for two main reasons. They stand nearest to the New Testament records and in many cases do little more than repeat the main features of the New Testament *lex orandi*. Many of them are characterized by a tradition of 'sober moralism' which was so notable a feature of late first-century and early second-century Christianity. The part played in this trend by writers like Clement and Hermas may perhaps suggest that it was a special concern of the Church at Rome during the period. It may represent the principal feature in nascent Christianity which made so strong an appeal to the 'God-fearer' or Gentile back-bencher of the Jewish synagogues of the Dispersion. S. James had his followers no less than S. Paul or S. John, unless indeed we are to accept the critical hypothesis which sees in the Epistle of S. James another second-century member of this school.[1]

The principal value of the Apostolic Fathers lies, however, just in their proximity to the New Testament law of prayer. Their main purpose was practical or devotional instruction rather than theological exposition. Even S. Ignatius, the most theological of them all, is in no sense a systematic thinker. It would, in fact, be a grave error in historical perspective to

[1] See for instance J. H. Ropes, *I.C.C.*; Moffatt, *Introduction to the New Testament.* But it is safer to retain a prudent agnosticism on the date and provenance of this mysterious Epistle.

expect from them more than is actually there—a simple exposition of the practical content of the Christian Faith. To regard them as the norm for all later theological development would be comparable to taking an elementary manual of Christian instruction, part intellectual but mainly devotional, designed for candidates for Confirmation, as the *ne plus ultra* of Christian theology. Many fall into this trap, but never wisely. It would be like getting caught psychologically at the 'teen age' and never growing up.

II. *The Apologists* take up the same theme, but lift it immediately to a more philosophical level. They represent the first generation of what would now be called 'Christian frontiersmen' concerned to get into real communication with the pagan world around them. In this capacity they sought to make the most of every point of contact with their pagan contemporaries. Thus they present Christianity as the new philosophy, and lay perhaps too little stress on the elements in Christianity which could not readily afford bridgeheads into paganism. What is unique tends to be passed over in preference to what could more readily be understood by those to whom their treatises were principally directed.

They were rather the first Christian philosophers than the first Christian theologians. Whether their personal faith was richer than their published writings must remain an unsolved problem. The *Apologies* of S. Justin might indeed suggest that it was so. It would, however, be difficult to deny that their avowed purpose to make Christianity intellectually respectable in a thought-climate largely alien to that in which it was born may well have determined their selection of the data upon which they rested their case. Christ the Teacher would make an immediate appeal to many who could only be baffled by more profound and complex ways in which the doctrine of Redemption could be stated.

III. *Clement of Alexandria.* Here the task of the Apologists is reinforced by a further task, which led to a convergent method and an identical conclusion, the struggle against Gnosticism. Clement as a Christian 'frontiersman' was concerned not only with attack from those who were unmistakably outside the Christian tradition, but also from those who claimed to be in some sense within it. His emphasis on the intellectual elements within Christianity was not merely an attempt to answer the needs of an *intellectus quaerens fidem*, but also an attempt to reabsorb those who found themselves attracted by the claims of Gnosticism to penetrate more deeply into the Christian realities themselves. His intellectualization of Christianity, while no doubt reflecting profoundly his own personal approach and character, was also closely bound up with both aspects of his particular task for the Church of his day.

To what, then, do these data really amount? There is no question that the concept of Christ the Teacher bringing as part of His Redemptive work for humanity Knowledge and Illumination is a basic element in the

Christian doctrine of Redemption. No doctrine of the Cross, for example, which does not explain how the world is made the better by it can claim to represent the fulness of the Christian tradition. Again, any theory which separates the obligation of leading a better life from the Redemption brought by Christ has small claim for acceptance by Christians. But it is quite another thing with authors like Harnack and Rashdall to regard this element within the whole Christian tradition as the only one which is authentic or which has necessarily pride of place. Still less can we regard it as a kind of theological 'restrictive practice.' Brunner, for one, in the few pages which he devotes to S. Irenaeus in his work *The Mediator* rightly protests against such tendencies.[1]

It is clear, then, that, though we are on firm ground in treating the concept of Christ the Example, Teacher, and Illuminator as the starting-point in our study of the patristic doctrine of Redemption, we may expect to have to travel further if we are to probe more deeply into the heart of their doctrine. Little will need to be unlearnt, but much added, if we are to discover the answer to the question *Cur Deus Homo?* given in the formative period of the development of doctrine in the undivided Church.

[1] op. cit., pp. 249–64.

CHAPTER III

CHRIST THE VICTOR AND THE DOCTRINE OF THE RECAPITULATIO

It is, perhaps, hard for modern man to realize how hag-ridden was the world into which Christ came. Anderson Scott,[1] however, has made it clear that among the elements which make up the Christian doctrine of Redemption is the concept of release from the cosmic forces which oppose mankind and its spiritual progress. Perhaps in a period in which economic insecurity, international disorder, and ideological conflict form the backcloth against which is set the life of ordinary people, we are better able than our fathers to enter with sympathy and understanding into the motives which led the early Christians to frame in these terms at least part of their teaching about the redemption wrought by our Lord. Some at least of the elements which the psychologist would describe by the concepts of complex, frustration, divided self-hood, and the like would be included under this rubric in the early centuries. The Fathers carry on with equal earnestness this part of the teaching of the New Testament. Belief in the existence of demons united Origen and his pagan opponent, Celsus.[2] The only

[1] C. Anderson Scott, *Christianity according to S. Paul*, pp. 28–38, quoting C. Moody, *Faith of the Early Converts*.
[2] Origen, *c. Cels.* vii. 67–70.

real difference between them was their exact status and the attitude which it is appropriate for men to take towards them. Celsus regards them as subordinate deities worthy of human worship, Origen as hostile powers besetting mankind but in principle overcome by Christ. Beside the 'regulars' of the demonic world, Satan, the Devil, Beelzebub and the like, there were the Pauline 'reinforcements' in the shape of personalized sin and death.

The doctrine of demons is regarded by S. Ignatius[1] as an integral, though slightly esoteric, part of the Christian tradition. Athenagoras includes it no less than the doctrine of the Trinity in his outline of Christian theology.[2] The Gnostic *Acts of Thomas*[3] mentions the doctrine of God, the Resurrection, the Holy Eucharist, and demons as fit subjects for Christian preaching. The list, however, represents rather a job lot of topics than the reasoned heads of a *Summa Theologia*. Whereas in the *Contra Celsum* Origen follows the lead of S. Ignatius in treating the devil as a somewhat esoteric theme, in the *De Principiis* he includes the doctrine of demons in preference to many themes which we might regard of greater importance and significance.[4] Evidently the doctrine formed part of the *lex orandi* which he here sets himself to expound.

It is the great merit of Aulén's work *Christus Victor* that it expounds the conviction that in the redeeming act of Christ mankind has been freed from the power of

---

[1] Ignatius, *Trall.* 5.   [2] Athenagoras, *Suppl.* 10.   [3] *Acts of Thomas*, 36.
[4] Origen, *De Princ.* i. 8. 1.

the demons as one of the great formative influences in the patristic doctrine of Redemption. He even goes so far as to term it the Classical Tradition of the subject.

Three points may be made with regard to this tradition:

I. Aulén himself calls attention to the fact that the Victory of Christ involves every part of His human life—His whole Incarnation as Living, Dying, and Rising again.[1] The thought of the hymn:

> Hallowed birth by being born
> Conquered death by dying

is true to the spirit of the *Christus Victor* tradition.

Recently, however, this part of his theme has been reinforced by Martin Werner's detailed analysis of the various parts of the life of our Lord which are mentioned as focal points in the Vicarious Victory of Christ.[2]

(*a*) *The Birth*. Origen makes the interesting point that the very Conception of the *Logos* as Man in the Virgin Womb necessitated a victory over the demons. To get into the world at all, the *Logos* had, as it were, to break through a *cordon insanitaire* of celestial powers.[3] From this part at least of the teaching of Origen, Methodius did not apparently dissent.[4] With this must also be associated the interpretation of the coming of the Magi given by S. Ignatius and S. Justin

[1] Aulén, *Christus Victor*, p. 48.
[2] M. Werner, *Die Entstehung des Christlichen Dogmas*, pp. 249–66.
[3] Origen, *c. Cels*. i. 60.   [4] Methodius, *Symp*. iii. 6.

as a victory over astrology rather than a homage rendered by astrology to the Infant Christ.[1]

(*b*) *The Temptations.* Here it is very clear that the Synoptists, and therefore presumably Jesus Himself, saw the Temptations in the desert as a victory over the devil. It represented indeed the first fall rather than the final overthrow. 'The devil departed from Him for a season.' This is familiar ground for which no special references to the Fathers need be given.

(*c*) *The Death of Christ.* Here again the significance lay right on the surface. The Fourth Gospel speaks of the 'prince of this world' as coming and having nothing in Christ.[2] S. Paul speaks of 'world rulers' who, if they had known, would not have crucified the Lord of Glory![3] The interpretation of this passage is not clear. It may mean Caiaphas, Herod, and Pilate, or it may refer rather to the cosmic powers which are believed to be concerned in the Death of Christ. There is a similar ambiguity in the interpretation of the passage by the Fathers. S. Cyprian and Lactantius accept the former interpretation,[4] while the *Ascension of Isaiah*, S. Ignatius, Tertullian, and probably Origen prefer the interpretation of the rulers as demonic forces.[5] Words like 'conquer' and 'destroy' are freely used by the Fathers in this connexion.[6] Christ is the

---

[1] Ignatius, *Eph.* xix. 1. Justin, *Dial.* lxxviii. 9. See an interesting article by W. K. Lowther Clarke in *Theology*, Vol. xxvii, pp. 72–80, entitled 'The Rout of the Magi.'

[2] John xiv. 30.   [3] 1 Cor. ii. 8.

[4] Cyprian, *Quod idola non sunt dii*, 14; Lactantius, *Div. Inst.* iv. 16.

[5] *Ascensio Isaiae* 9, 14; Ignatius, *Eph.* xix. 1; Tertullian, *Adv. Marc.* v. 6; Origen, *De Princ.* iii. 2, 1; Cyril Jerus., *Orat. Cat.* xii. 15.

[6] Justin (νικᾶν); Irenaeus ('vincere').

slayer of Death himself.[1] A typical phrasing of this idea occurs in the little-known *Altercatio Simonis et Theophili*: 'For this purpose at His first Advent Christ was slain to free us from the power of the devil and the worship of idols.'[2]

(*d*) *The Resurrection.* The Fathers never treat the Death and Resurrection of Christ in isolation from each other. The saving pattern of the Incarnation includes both these facts as vital moments. Thus Origen is typical of many others when he writes: 'Through His Resurrection He destroyed the Kingdom of Death, whence it is written that He freed captivity.'[3]

(*e*) *The Descent into Hades.* The New Testament emphasis upon the Descent into Hades probably lay rather upon the preaching to the spirits in prison than upon the victory over demonic powers. In certain passages in the Fathers, however, this significance is also present. The vocabulary of violence, from robbery to earthquake, is used to express the shattering effect upon the demons of our Lord's Descent *ad inferos*.[4] It is interesting to catch an allusion to the binding of the strong man in the vocabulary of the passage.[5] The 'Origenistic Tractate' edited by Batiffol has a characteristic phrase: 'The whole power of impure spirits an unnumerable number of enemies was there

---

[1] Aphraates, *Dem.* xxii. 4; Athanasius, *de Inc.* xxx. 2; Cyril Jerus. *Orat Cat.* xiv. 19 has a graphic expression of this truth.

[2] *Altercatio Simonis et Theophili*, vi. 24.

[3] Origen, *in Rom.* v. 1; Epiphanius, *Haer.* xlii. 12, 3.

[4] *Acts of Thomas*, 10 (καταστρέφειν, σαδεύειν). *Tract. Orig.* (edit. Batiffol), p. 154 ('*exterminare*,' '*perdere*'), Hippolytus, *Church Order* (quoted by H. Lietzmann, *Messe und Herrenmahl*, p. 42 '*solvere*,' '*calcare*'); *Test. Dom.* I. 28 ('*captivum ducere*'); Hilary Poict. *de Trin.* iv. 42 ('*captivum ducere*').

[5] Matt. xii. 29.

overthrown.'¹ The Gospel of Nicodemus even records the demons' cry of defeat: 'We are defeated; woe is us!'² The devil is bound hand and foot.

(*f*) *The Ascension.* Here Scriptural warrant could be found in Ephesians iv. 8, based upon the Septuagint text of Psalm lxvii. 19. It is referred to as the place of victory over the demons by S. Justin,³ but it reaches greater development among the later Gnostics. The Redeemer breaks through the surrounding ring of demons, the superterrestrial rulers or *archontes*, on His way back from earth to heaven. This is really the exact obverse of the theory of Origen that the *Logos* had to defeat the demons in order to get into the world at all. Demons here oppose, not the Descent to Earth but the Return to Heaven.

The centrality of this aspect of the doctrine of Redemption can scarcely be overestimated. It occurs in a general form in most early Fathers. S. Justin speaks of the demons as being made subject to His Name and the dispensation of His impending Death.⁴ It is the principal answer given by S. Irenaeus to the question *Cur Deus Homo?* 'That He might slay sin, render death null and void, and give life to man.'⁵ The matter is expressed in a similar fashion in his other extant work: 'The Word of God was made flesh in order that He might destroy death and bring us to life, for we were tied and bound in sin, we were born

---

¹ *Tract. Orig.* (ed. Batiffol), p. 153 ff.
² *Ev. Nicod.* vi (xxii).   ³ Justin, *Dial.* 36.
⁴ ibid., 30.
⁵ Irenaeus, *Adv. Haer. Omn.* iii. 19, 6 (Harvey ii, p. 103), '*ut occideret peccatum, evacuaret autem mortem, et vivificaret hominem.*'

in sin and lived under the dominion of death.'[1] Again, 'Christ began to slay sin and to redeem guilty man so that sin should be killed by man, and man go forth free from death.'[2] Paul of Samosata speaks of our Lord as becoming holy and righteous by conflict and toil overcoming the sins of our forefather.[3] Here the mythology is less apparent though the idea of victory is equally clear. Origen sees the death of Christ as the beginning and progress of the destruction of the Evil One.[4] In the visible crucifixion of Christ, the devil and all his princes and powers were invisibly crucified.[5] S. Cyril of Jerusalem teaches his candidates for Holy Baptism that Jesus 'bore the sins of the world and died that, having slain sin, He might raise thee up in righteousness.' Such quotations might be multiplied almost indefinitely, but they will, perhaps, serve as typical references to the doctrine in the works of representative Fathers.

II. The second feature of interest with regard to the *Christus Victor* theory is the way in which it handles the problem of dualism, which we have seen already to be deeply involved in this tradition. Clearly a theory which leans so heavily on the side of dualism must be careful to avoid splitting the Universe between God and the devil. S. Irenaeus is naturally concerned with this problem in view of the absolute dualism of most of the systems against which he was writing. There appear to be two main ways in which he tries to vindi-

[1] ibid., *Epid.* 37.   [2] ibid., *Adv. Haer. Omn.* iii. 19, 6 (Harvey ii, p. 101).
[3] Paul of Samosata (Loofs), p. 339.   [4] Origen, *c. Cels.* vii. 17.
[5] ibid., *Hom. in Josh.* viii. 3.

cate the moral character of Christ's Victory over the devil. According to the first, the devil has no title in man. He is a usurper, a tyrant, a robber, unjustly laying hands upon what does not concern him, and therefore deserving to be dispossessed as unceremoniously as possible.

There were clearly excellent reasons why so strong an anti-Gnostic and anti-Marcionite Father as S. Irenaeus should wish at all costs to avoid too close an association with the dualism which was the attendant circumstance of the one, and the mainspring of the other. The single, entire, and undivided control of all things by the supreme God is as vital a theme to him as the identity of the God of creation with that of Redemption and the unity of the saving pattern which underlies all His works. Yet at the same time S. Irenaeus seeks to vindicate the ethical character of God by showing that even with the usurper God observes the rules of fair play. He avoids mere external compulsion or blind force, even where He might legitimately be expected to use it. God deals according to justice even with apostasy itself. Behind the obscure language about Redemption *secundum suadelam* lies the victorious self-donation of Christ for man and the redemption which He thereby won.[1] There is as yet little trace of the idea of ransom from the devil as it is unfolded in the writings of some later Fathers.

In Tertullian this theme of relative dualism is at once legalized and coarsened. The devil possesses

[1] Irenaeus, *Adv. Haer. Omn.* v. 1, 1 (Harvey ii, p. 315).

natural rights or just dominion over sinners, though this does not extend over the household of God.[1] It is reasonable that God should resume His control over His own image and similitude which had been so unjustly taken captive by the devil[2] by a converse operation. Rashdall interprets this passage as meaning 'by a rival fraud,' but the idea of fraud is rather read into than derived from the Latin, and it is more probable that, obscure though it is, the phrase represents rather an echo of the recapitulation theory to which we shall turn our attention later in the chapter.

There is a passage in Origen which for the first time contains *in extenso*[3] the idea of the deceit of the devil. It may be translated somewhat as follows:

But to Whom did Christ give His soul for ransom? Surely not to God. Could it then be to the Evil One? For he had us in his power until the ransom for us should be given to him, even the life of Christ. The Evil One had been deceived and led to suppose that he was capable of mastering the soul and did not see that to hold Him involved a trial of strength greater than he could successfully undertake. Therefore death, though he thought that he had prevailed against Him, no longer prevails against Him. Christ, then, having become free among the dead and stronger than the power of death and so much stronger than death, that all who will among those who are mastered by death may follow Him, death no longer prevailing against them. For everyone who is with Jesus is stronger than death.[4]

[1] Tertullian, *De Fuga*, 2, where '*propria potestas*' may be translated 'natural right.'
[2] ibid., *De carne Christi*, 17, '*aemula operatione.*'
[3] I am, however, reminded that a bare allusion to the deception of the devil occurs in Ignatius, *Eph.* 19.
[4] Origen, *Com. in Math.* xvi. 8.

At first sight the passage would seem rather to belong to the Christ Victim theme, but a less cursory reading will show that the theme of victory over death and the devil is really uppermost in the writer's mind. Rashdall offers a vigorous defence of the passage.[1] It contains little of the offensive features of the ransom theory in later writings. The metaphor is drawn not from the law court, but from the battlefield. Ransom is repurchase rather than penalty, and it does not stand as the only attempt in the writings of Origen to expound the significance of the death of Christ. All these observations are, of course, true and reinforce the conclusion already drawn that it must be interpreted along the lines of the *Christus Victor* theory. But it is certainly odd to find Rashdall, stout moralist as he was, defending the notion of the deception of the devil contained in the passage. 'There is nothing really grotesque or unethical, irreligious or unphilosophical' in the passage. To Rashdall it means little more than a statement that Divine Providence allows wicked men to compass their own destruction by underestimating the strength of the forces ranged against them. This may or may not be implied in the passage, but it is not what Origen restricts himself to saying. Rashdall seeks to exculpate Origen on rather too easy terms. It is one thing to say (quite truly!) that the devil fails by overestimating his own strength. It is quite another thing to assert, as Origen plainly does, that the devil is deceived by God. We may well agree that many refinements of this theme are

[1] Rashdall, *Idea of Atonement*, pp. 259–61.

mercifully absent from the passage. What is present is difficult enough. Clearly, however, despite the somewhat unfortunate imagery, the passage still belongs in the main to the *Christus Victor* tradition.

This type of thinking is further developed in the *Great Catechetical Oration* of S. Gregory of Nyssa. Here the concept of the deception of the devil almost, but not quite, takes control of the whole passage at the expense of the theme of vicarious victory. Any fisherman, however, will realize that the note of victory is not wholly removed from the analogy which forms its central theme. Christ serves as our counterpart in a transaction to which both the devil and God agree and which therefore can be considered just. The devil, however, finds that in accepting the bargain he has made a grave miscalculation. The counterpart to ourselves is not what he expected. He had reckoned upon Christ as being merely a man like ourselves. Instead he finds Him to be the God-Man, the Giver of immortality Who could not therefore be held by death. Here is introduced the main metaphor, that of the bait and the fish-hook. The devil gulps down the bait represented by the humanity of our Lord and is left caught and hanging on the hook with the Divine *Logos* playing the line.

The Deity was hidden under the veil of our nature, that, as is done by greedy fish, the hook of the Deity might be gulped down along with the bait of the flesh and thus life being introduced into the house of death and light shining in the darkness, that which is contradictory to light and life might vanish away; for it is not in the nature of darkness to remain where light is present or of death to exist where life is present.[1]

S. Gregory shows himself aware of the moral problems involved, which he tries to meet first by insisting that there is nothing unreasonable about the deceiver being himself deceived, and secondly by suggesting (following a hint from Origen concerning the ultimate salvability of the devil) that the deception might possibly in the long run work out to the advantage of the devil himself. He might have noted that the fisherman jerks the fish upward in his victorious playing of the line! The background, though it is only a background in the passage, is still the *Christus Victor* tradition. The references to the conflict between light and darkness, life and death, prove as much. A struggle between God and the devil is going on with no holds barred which the devil started himself and cannot therefore complain if his tactics of deception are turned against himself.

The protests against the theory of the deception of the devil are of greater interest than the sub-forms of the theory itself. The anonymous author of the tractate *De Recta Fide*, long attributed to Origen himself, accuses the theory of being Marcionite in basis. He has correctly noted the dualist character of the *Christus Victor* theory though he is not fully alive to the relative character of its underlying character. His protest runs as follows:

He that was sold, you say was the Christ? Who was the seller? Did the simple myth come down to you that he

[1] op. cit. 17–23.

who sells and he who buys are brethren? If the devil being bad is sold to the good, he is not bad, but good; for he that of old envied man is now no longer impelled by envy, handing over his authority to the good. He then who has ceased from envy and all manner of evil will be righteous. God then Himself is found to be the seller. The truth is rather that men who have alienated themselves on account of their sins were ransomed by His loving-kindness.[1]

Here follows an account of the origin of evil, written from the libertarian point of view, and an insistence in the spirit of the Fourth Gospel that Christ gave rather than sold His life on our behalf. The writer continues:

The devil, then, holds the blood of Christ as the purchase price of Man? What immense and blasphemous folly. He laid down what He took. What sort of a sale is this?

Harnack[2] describes the argument as no less acute than true and victorious. This depends, however, on the form of theory which he is criticizing, or whether he has really understood its implications at the outset. The myth that he who sells and he who buys are brethren (probably a proverb of the 'birds of a feather flock together' type), though a vital part of the argument, really has nothing to do with the case. The argument is valid against a purely mercantile theory which regards the death of Christ as a mere mechanical transaction, but if the basis of the original argument was some more or less mythologically embroidered form of the *Christus Victor*, the author

---

[1] Ps. Adamantius, *Dial. de Recta Fide*, i. 27.
[2] Harnack, *History of Dogmas*, English translation, Vol. ii, p. 291.

has not really got to grips with the argument which he is criticizing.

A second critique of the theory of ransom is contained in the rather obscure language of a theological poem. S. Gregory of Nazianzus, its author, writes as follows:

> I ask to Whom was the blood of Christ outpoured? If to the Evil One, alas, what belongs to Christ is offered to the Evil One. But if you say to God, how can this be when we were in the grip of another? The ransom belongs to the one who holds the other captive. Can it be true that He offers a sacrifice to God in order that God Himself should snatch us from our captor and receive the Christ as an equivalent for one who has fallen? For the Anointer of Christ is not capable of being taken captive. That is what we think, but we respect the types of divine things.[1]

The last sentence shows alike that S. Gregory realizes that he is dealing with analogies and that they have become almost traditional in his own day. Certainly his friend, S. Gregory of Nyssa, shows no compunction about using them. It is, however, hard to believe that he has really grasped the significance of the views which he criticizes. His argument against the ransom being offered to God is certainly valid, but apart from an ejaculatory 'alas,' he never considers the alternative which really characterizes the *Christus Victor* school. 'Alas that that which belongs to Christ should be offered to the devil,' he complains. 'Alas indeed,' S. Gregory of Nyssa or others of his type could reply, 'but that is just the sort of paradoxical situation produced by human sin.'

[1] Gregory of Nazianzus, *Carmen Theol.* x. 65 f.

The really important point about these mythological theories which has made it worth while to examine them in some detail is that it is not enough to dismiss them as mythological and immoral elements repugnant to the modern man, as Rashdall and Harnack tended to do, without trying to set them against their appropriate background and to make a serious effort to assess their real value. They all appear to be analogical attempts to express—with varying degrees of success—the relative character of the dualism which characterizes the *Christus Victor* theory. The problem which they set themselves to answer is a real one, the nature and status of the dualism involved in the very act of Redemption itself. They may have been less successful than the modern theologian in offering an answer to the problem. Picture-thinking, with all its advantages in expressing imponderables, has its own corresponding limitations, and can never in any case serve as a substitute for the best and most rigorous exercise of the faculty for exact thinking. But at least they asked the right question, and the nerve of all their answers reveals quite clearly that they were struggling to express as vividly and clearly as they could the principle that the devil, for all his startling successes at the expense of humanity, is a revolted subject and not an independent being dividing the sovereignty of the world with God by nature and of right. The devil, like our systems, has his little day, but will finally by the act of God in Christ, at first in principle and then in actuality, be brought to naught.

III. The third point of interest in the *Christus Victor* theory and its variants lies in the background of Christology against which it is set. Just as we found that the 'exemplarist' passages which we considered in the last chapter could be divided between those which took as their starting point the life and death of 'Jesus good above all others' and those who had their focus in the *Logos Paidagogos*, so the *Christus Victor* tradition can be further divided into those views which see as the Victor the Incarnate Lord and those which may be described as offering a *Logos Victor* variation of this theme.

The former Christological variant of *Christus Victor* thinking is closely linked to the doctrine of the Recapitulation. The New Testament sources for this are Pauline: Ephesians i. 10,[1] and the Adam-Christ parallelism in Romans and 1 Corinthians. The exact significance of the word is not wholly easy to determine. Its Greek original is Ἀνακεφαλάιωσις. The word κεφάλαιον which underlies the second half of the word means 'summary,' and the whole word might therefore imply little more than the summation of all things in Christ in accordance with the picture given in the later Pauline Epistles. On the other hand, the preposition ἀνὰ with which the word opens should suggest renewal or repetition. The idea of restoration is never far absent from the meaning of the word, although the Latin translation *recapitulatio*, so frequent in the Latin version of S. Irenaeus, would never by

[1] F. Loofs alone refuses to see Ephesians i. 10 one of the sources of the term here.

itself suggest this. The relation between Christ and
Adam which the word contains is something more
than mere analogy, something less than strict identity.
For Bousset[1] the word involves a whole theology,
combining the idea of human evolution from below
with Divine intervention from above. But this is
probably much too subtle, although the background
of the word suggests not obscurely the idea that
Christ is the focal point of human history. The
meaning of 'restoration by repetition' is probably not
far from the truth.

The word first occurs to our knowledge in a passage
of S. Justin[2] quoted by S. Irenaeus, but it is the latter
who made it a central theme in his own theology.
The collocation of S. Justin and S. Irenaeus suggested
to Loofs that the term was part of the theological
heritage of Asia Minor, but this, though possible, can
hardly be called proved.[3] The term is not merely
applied to our Lord; S. Irenaeus also speaks of the
Anti-Christ as making a *recapitulatio* of universal
iniquity and deceit.[4]

Three elements seem to be included in the theme:

(i) *Restoration.* S. Irenaeus never tires of emphasizing the unity of mind and purpose behind Creation
and Redemption. It formed an important part of his
defence against Gnosticism and Marcionism. The

---

[1] W. Bousset quoted by F. H. Lawson, *The Biblical Theology of S. Irenaeus*,
p. 142.
[2] Irenaeus, *Adv. Haer. Omn.* iv. 11, 2 (Harvey ii, p. 159), quoting Justin,
'*suum plasma recapitulans.*'
[3] F. Loofs, *Theophilus von Antiochien*, pp. 357–68; *Leitfaden*, p. 145.
[4] Irenaeus, *Adv. Haer. Omn.* v. 25, 1 (Harvey ii, p. 391); v. 29, 2 (Harvey
ii, p. 405).

term 'recapitulation' acts as a bridge term between creation and redemption. Christ, Who recapitulates the ancient Creation in Himself,[1] thereby restores to Man by His obedience whatever the Primal Man lost by his disobedience. Adam's sin lost for mankind the similitude of God and the right to communion with Him. Yet even in the days of his fall, Adam never escaped the hands of his Creator, and in Christ mankind has once again restored to it its original pattern.

(ii) *Summation.* Christ, the victorious recapitulator of humanity, embodies in Himself the long course of human history as purposed by God in His original Creation. Clearly such an idea is inevitable if the action of Christ is to affect others besides Himself. 'He recapitulated in Himself the long evolution of human history.'[2] The Word came through the whole dispensation of God recapitulating all things in Himself.[3] His work can thus be described as a compendium.[4] If His single act were to have the same universal range which the sin of Adam was held to possess some such conception must be a necessary ingredient in the doctrine of salvation by Recapitulation.

(iii) *Iteration.* But this conception involves the consequence that Christ should go over the whole human process again, albeit in compendium, victor-

---

[1] Irenaeus, *Adv. Haer. Omn.* iii. 31, 3 (Harvey ii, p. 121), '*Antiquam plasmationem in se recapitulans.*'

[2] ibid., iii. 19, 1 (Harvey ii, p. 95), '*longam hominum expositionem in seipso recapitulans.*'

[3] ibid., iii. 17, 6 (Harvey ii, p. 87), '*Veniens per universam dispositionem et omnia in semetipso recapitulans.*'

[4] ibid., iii. 19, 1 (Harvey ii, p. 95), '*in compendio nobis salutem praestans.*' The original adverb in the Greek may have been συντόμως.

iously where Adam was defeated. This is the element in the doctrine which is most noticeably to the fore in the work of S. Irenaeus. Its sources, though still Pauline, are rather Romans and 1 Corinthians than Ephesians. Christ shares all the experiences of humanity, sin only excepted. 'For this reason He became like man an infant, although He was perfect, not on His own account, but because of the infancy of man.'[1] Even His birth has certain affinities with that of Adam. If Adam was born of virgin soil, Christ was born of a pure Virgin 'keeping the similitude.'[2] His human struggles make Him a veritable *Christus Agonistes*, for 'He was man contending for the Fathers and paying for disobedience by His own obedience.'[3] The parallelism even extends to the Cross: 'Dissolving that human disobedience which was originally committed in respect of a Tree, healing it by His obedience upon a Tree.'[4]

The analogy even goes further, and is worked out in relation to the Blessed Virgin Mary and primeval Woman. The parallel was not first drawn by S. Irenaeus, nor was he the last to exploit it theologically.[5] 'The knot of the disobedience of Eve was untied by the obedience of Mary, for what Eve bound up by her unbelief, the Virgin Mary released by her

---

[1] ibid., iv. 63, 1 (Harvey ii., p. 295), '*et propter hoc co-infantiatium est homini Verbum Dei cum esset perfectus non propter se sed propter hominis infantiam.*'

[2] ibid., iii. 31, 1 (Harvey ii, pp. 120-1), especially note '*servata similitudine.*'

[3] ibid., iii. 19, 5 (Harvey ii, p. 100), '*Luctatus est et vicit; erat enim homo pro patribus certans, et per obedientiam inobedientiam persolvens.*'

[4] ibid., v. 16, 2 (Harvey ii, p. 368), '*eam quae in ligno facta fuerat inobedientiam per eam quae in ligno fuerat obedientiam sanans.*'

[5] Justin, *Dial.* 100. Tertullian, *De carne Christi*, 17.

faith.'[1] Mr. Lawson, in a recent book on the Biblical theology of S. Irenaeus, describes the Virgin Mary as a Subsidiary Champion and notes that the doctrine receives later developments which would certainly have been foreign to the mind of S. Irenaeus himself. It is, however, possible that it is going beyond the evidence to describe the Blessed Virgin as a 'Subsidiary Champion.' There is a significant distinction of term between the rôle of our Lord and of His Blessed Mother. The one is described as recapitulation, the other merely as recirculation. The wheel has come full circle and the path which Eve trod in one way Mary retraced in the opposite direction. The doctrine occurs in later Fathers like Tertullian and, characteristically enough, in S. Methodius, but little is added to the profundity of its conception in S. Irenaeus.

Its significance in his writings cannot easily be overestimated. The close relation which it asserts between Creation and Redemption and the identity of pattern which it unfolds in each process lends great strength and richness to what is, after all, the fundamental basis of his answer to the question, *Cur Deus Homo?* Whether indeed S. Irenaeus himself appreciated all the adumbrations of a Christian philosophy of history which some of his expositors have found in this circle of ideas may reasonably be doubted; at least they do not lie far below the surface. An evolutionary purpose

---

[1] Irenaeus, *Adv. Haer. Omn.* iii. 32, 1 (Harvey ii, p. 124), '*Sic autem et Evae inobedientiae nodus solutionem accepit per obedientiam Mariae. Quod enim alligavit virgo Eva per incredulitatem, hoc virgo Maria solvit per fidem.*' The parallel is worked in detail in H. Koch, *Virgo Maria, Virgo Eva.*

in history, a Divine inbreaking into history, a crucial experiment in which what Luther called the 'proper man' reversed a process which had mysteriously grown like a snowball since the sin of Adam, are all themes suggested by the word itself and its immediate associations. What is of special importance for our present purpose is, however, to call attention to the rich positive valuation which is given to the humanity of the Incarnate Lord. It is not the Word, but the Word in His humanity, Who is the subject of the *recapitulatio*. We are still clearly within the range of the *Christus Victor* tradition: 'If man had not conquered the adversary of man, the enemy would not have been justly conquered; again, if God had not given the salvation, we should not have securely obtained it, and if man had not been united to God, he could not have obtained incorruptibility.'[1] The two-sidedness of the *Christus Victor* tradition to which Aulén repeatedly calls attention could not have been more clearly expressed.

But the advancing tide of *Logos* Christology, which is such a marked feature of the period which followed the life and times of S. Irenaeus, inevitably meant that the *Christus Victor* tradition would be at least modified in the direction of, or even replaced by, a *Logos Victor* tradition. The complaint of Apollinarius[2] that the death of a man, even if followed by the Resurrection, could not in itself destroy death, is not only fatal to the dualist Christology against which he was primarily

[1] Irenaeus, *Adv. Haer. Omn.* iii. 19, 6 (Harvey ii, p. 100).
[2] Apollinarius, *Frag.* 95 (Lietzmann, p. 228).

protesting, but also was not destined to leave the *Christus Victor* tradition unaffected. It would be fatal to the Christology of Paul of Samosata, Diodore, and Flavian; it would also affect the Irenaean emphasis upon a redemption which occurred primarily in and through the humanity of the One Christ. A Christ victorious in His humanity could save only His own soul by His righteousness. The idea of compendious recapitulation would not be enough for the devotees of a *Logos* Christology. Only if the Mighty Victor were the *Logos* of God could Redemption be transmitted to all mankind.

For S. Athanasius, who still belongs to the tradition of Vicarious Victory, it is the incorruptible *Logos* who restores to us what we have lost through the sin of Adam. The passage from S. Gregory of Nyssa analysed earlier in this chapter proves that by contrast with S. Irenaeus the value of the manhood of our Lord has become instrumental only. Instead of being a fundamental element of first-class religious importance for the act of Redemption, it has become only a necessary bridgehead into humanity to provide a possible *point d'appui* for the conflict with the devil. If the metaphor of the bait is in any sense to be treated seriously it must imply that the humanity of our Lord was little more than a peculiarly tempting example of the kind of food with which the devil was already sadly familiar. This is a far cry from the rich positive religious sense of the value of the humanity of our Lord which underlies the *recapitulatio* terminology

and the authentic strands of the *Christus Victor* tradition. By this time, however, a further theory of
Redemption had become more deeply associated with
the *Logos* tradition, that of physical and mystical
redemption by deification, and it is to this that we must
next turn our attention.

CHAPTER IV

CHRIST THE GIVER OF INCORRUPTION AND DEIFICATION

IT is extremely difficult to give a coherent account of this part of the patristic doctrine of Redemption because the principal words involved are patent of many different nuances. Even within the compass of the writings of any one particular Father, it is difficult to ascertain whether terms like 'incorruption' or 'immortality' have primarily an eschatological, physical, metaphysical, or mystical significance. The lexicography of the subject is full of pitfalls even for the expert.

Many background issues are involved which add to the number of 'concomitant variables.' The nature of man before and after the Fall, the character and endowments of Primal Man, the exact deprivation which the Fall involved,—all enter into the picture.

The New Testament background is relatively slight. The Pastoral Epistles refer to God 'Who only hath immortality'[1] and the late pseudepigraph, 2 Peter, contains what is really the proof-text of the whole tradition, the prayer 'that ye may become partakers of the Divine Nature having escaped the corruption ($\phi\theta o\rho\grave{a}$) that is in the world through lust.'[2]

Four main variants of this tradition occur in the

[1] 1 Tim. vi. 16.   [2] 2 Pet. i. 4.

patristic period; two of which seem to have special connexion with the Historic Christ, while the other two rather focus attention upon the Divine *Logos*, though associated in some measure also with His Incarnation. The first group contains views in which the eschatological dimension is clearly dominant, with little or no reference to the Fall or its effects. The second, closely connected in many cases with the doctrine of recapitulation, accepts a relatively 'light' view of the Fall and its consequences, and sees even these as neutralized by the assumption in the Incarnation of humanity, and the almost physical recapture of human possibilities. The second pair of views move away from these eschatological and quasi-physical starting points towards the metaphysical and the mystical. The former sees in the Redemption brought through the *Logos* the endowment of humanity with the metaphysical fulness of the Being of God, while the latter describes the goal of Redemption as Deification brought about by the close association with the Deifying *Logos* through His Humanity.

(i) The eschatological emphasis, though never completely purged from Christianity, is at its maximum with the Apostolic Fathers. As N. P. Williams[1] pointed out, their writings are characterized by an almost complete absence of preoccupation with the Fall and its consequences. In their view the Redeemer has provided the fulness of eschatological or Messianic Blessedness which, while beginning in a measure here and now, will only receive its perfect fruition hereafter.

[1] N. P. Williams, *The Doctrine of the Fall and Original Sin*, pp. 171–3.

71

Thus the *Didache* speaks of Christ as having revealed knowledge, faith, and immortality.[1] The Eucharist is spiritual food and drink to Eternal Life.[2] Christians are partakers in the immortal and imperishable,[3] though this appears to be restricted to the saints who alone will rise.[4] Barnabas, too, looks forward to Eternal Life after the Resurrection.[5] I Clement speaks of the Eternal *Gnosis*, by which he appears to mean the teaching which alone will ensure immortality.[6] II Clement seems to express the same idea by a hendiadys—Life and Incorruptibility.[7] So far, Immortality, Incorruptibility, and Eternal Life are almost controvertible terms; and the emphasis is upon promise for the future rather than enjoyment in the present. If we describe this form of the tradition as eschatological, it is not with a view to denying the continuance of eschatological ideas and concepts at a later stage, but rather to emphasizing that here they provide the principal category of theological interpretation. Later Fathers, without denying the eschatological as part of the Christian *lex orandi*, work with more complex and developed key-concepts.

(ii) The term 'physical' has become almost a technical term among historians of doctrine since the early years of the present century in which it was widely used by Harnack and Loofs. The latter offers a definition: 'The physical theory is the concept of Redemption as the removal of corruption through the union of Godhead and manhood fulfilled through

---

[1] *Didache*, ix. 3.   [2] ibid., x. 2–3.   [3] ibid., iv. 8.   [4] ibid., xvi. 6–8.
[5] *Barnabas*, viii. 5.   [6] *I Clement*, xxxvi. 2.   [7] *II Clement*, vi. 6.

Christ.'[1] It may be added that this quasi-physical redemption is frequently regarded as mediated through participation in the sacramental system. Its relation to the recapitulation doctrine may be regarded as fundamental. Harnack[2] tends almost to regard the term as one of theological abuse, and speaks as though it necessarily involved a materialization of the whole process of redemption. This is gratuitous, and those who accept different sacramental principles from those of Harnack will find the term merely a convenient description of the mediation through material agencies, incarnational and sacramental, of the salvation which Christ brought.

Loofs finds this theory (like that of the recapitulation noted above) a theological speciality of Asia Minor.[3] It would not be surprising if this were true, but the truth or error of this conjecture depends upon a number of questions outside the range of this inquiry. In S. Ignatius we find two elements for such a physical theory—a rich positive valuation of our Lord's humanity, and the concept of the Eucharist as the medicine of immortality, the antidote to death.[4] Loofs comments that this passage may not be quite as materialistic as it sounds, but its physical basis is clear enough.[5] The same theme recurs in the teaching of S. Irenaeus on the Eucharist: 'So our bodies receiving the Eucharist are no longer corruptible, having the hope of the Resurrection.'[6]

[1] Loofs, *Leitfaden zur Dogmengeschichte*, p. 203 n.
[2] Harnack, *History of Dogmas* (English translation), Vol. ii, pp. 239, etc.
[3] Loofs, *Leitfaden*, i. c.   [4] Ignatius, *Eph.* xx. 2.   [5] Loofs, *Leitfaden*, p. 101.
[6] Irenaeus, *Adv. Haer. Omn.* iv. 31, 4 (Harvey ii, p. 206).

With S. Irenaeus the underlying conceptions of this theory become considerably clearer. While not losing sight of the eschatological dimension of Redemption, his general theory looks backwards rather than forwards, to what Man has lost through the Fall rather than to what Man will one day receive in the Consummation. He is the first Father to make more than an incidental reference to the Fall. N. P. Williams[1] rightly regards him as the first systematizer of a 'light' doctrine of the Fall and its effects. Man as he came from the 'Hands of God' was a Dawn Man, an inchoate and unformed creature. S. Irenaeus expressly states that 'Man the Lord of the earth was but small, for he was a child, and it was necessary that he should grow and so come to his perfection.'[2] His sin was rather a deviation laterally than a Fall vertically, the groping after a wrong path rather than the apostasy of a saint. The Fall did not deprive him of the Image, but only of the Similitude of God, a deprivation serious enough, involving the loss of incorruptibility and immortality, but not involving total depravity. 'Adam never escaped from the Hands of God.'[3]

The restoration of these attributes is involved in the Redemptive Act of God. For this to be effective two processes must be set in motion. God must be united to manhood, and manhood must consequently be restored to communion with God. The process by which the Word of God was conceived to have become united to humanity has already been treated sufficiently

---

[1] N. P. Williams, *Doctrine of the Fall and Original Sin*, pp. 200-1.
[2] Irenaeus, *Epideixis*, 12.
[3] ibid., *Adv. Haer. Omn.* v. 1, 3 (Harvey ii, p. 317).

in our previous discussion of the recapitulation. Redemption is thus conceived as the reunion of two entities unnaturally separated by human sin. But the process must be completed by our restored communion with God. These two aspects are clearly set out in two passages. The first describes how Christ 'out of His great love became what we are, that He might make us what He is Himself';[1] the second insists that 'if man had not been united to God, he could have had no share in incorruptibility.'[2] Jules Gross[3] sees in these two passages taken together a sketch of the physical or mystical doctrine of deification. So confused are the terms in which the discussion is set that the two can be regarded as identical by an excellent scholar. This juxtaposition of apparently contrary adjectives, surprising enough at first sight, may serve to warn us that for S. Irenaeus the physical aspect of the doctrine tends to pass almost imperceptibly into the mystical plane. Physical realities underlie the theory—the assumption of real manhood by the Word, and the appropriation by the Christian of the benefits of this act through participation in the Eucharist—but their effects have nothing of the mechanical or the automatic about them. The goal and result is mystical even if the means are physical. S. Irenaeus with his splendid picture of the Living

---

[1] ibid., v, Praef. (Harvey ii, p. 314), '*Qui propter immensam suam dilectionem factus est quod sumus uti nos perficeret esse quod est ipse.*'

[2] ibid., iii. 19, 6 (Harvey ii, p. 100).

[3] Jules Gross, *La Divinisation du chrétien d'après les pères grecs*, p. 151. My indebtedness to this study for much of the material discussed in this chapter is gratefully acknowledged.

Man as the Glory of God[1] has no tendency to believe either that God will save us apart from, or despite, ourselves, or that, having saved us, we shall become other than ourselves. His insight into the fundamental essence of Redemption might perhaps be expressed by the prayer: 'Make us, we beseech Thee, living men.'

So far we have been able to trace a coherent rationale of the doctrine of Redemption on the basis of a quasi-physical theory of its causes and effects. There also occur, however, in his writings advances which were destined to have important consequences for the future. He is the first Father, for example, to associate the recovery of Incorruption directly with the Passion. 'By His Passion the Lord destroyed death, dissipated error, rooted out corruption, destroyed ignorance, displayed life, showed truth, and conferred incorruptibility.'[2] Here we may see the influence of the *Christus Victor* tradition of thinking, with its strong emphasis upon the importance of the Incarnation as a whole, and of the Passion in particular. Again, we may trace in his writings the germs of later developments of the doctrine of deification. He does not indeed use the actual term, but 'filiation,' the adoption of sons, certainly occurs. It is evident that here he prefers to follow the vocabulary of S. Paul rather than that of 2 Peter. 'The Word became man in order to make us what He is Himself.'[3] The idea of deification is clearly present, but it is almost as if a reverential

---

[1] Irenaeus, *Adv. Haer. Omn.* iv. 34, 7 (Harvey ii, p. 219), '*Gloria enim Dei vivens homo; vita autem hominis Visio Dei;* iv. 25, 1 (Harvey ii, p. 184), '*Haec enim gloria hominis perseverare ac permanere in Dei servitudine.*'
[2] ibid., ii. 32, 2 (Harvey i, p. 323).
[3] ibid., v, Praef. (Harvey ii, p. 314).

glottal-stop prevents the use of the actual term. Other and later writers in this tradition will be less overcome by godly fear in the matter!

(iii) A metaphysical variation of this tradition begins with the Greek Apologists and continues in the Alexandrine Fathers, slightly modified in the direction of mysticism. Their special preoccupation with the defensive presentation of Christianity in terms of Greek philosophy naturally led their thoughts in this direction. It has often been pointed out that these Fathers expressed the metaphysical fulness of being of God in terms of metaphysical negatives denying in Him the limitations of Being which belong to the created world. Immortality and incorruptibility are attributes of this character which man only partakes through his relation to and connexion with God. The Apologists are by no means agreed upon whether man ever possesses these endowments as of right. S. Justin, while noting that God intended to preserve man from corruption, denies the natural immortality of the human spirit[1] on the interesting ground that since immortality belongs of right to God alone, man, if he were immortal, would be not man but God. A similar doctrine of immortality may be found in Tatian who, while still maintaining that incorruptibility belongs only to God, believed that man received it by participation in the portion of God through the linking or association of the Divine Spirit with the human soul.'[2] Man is by himself

[1] Justin, *Dial.* 88; *De Res.* 8 (but the attribution of the latter treatise to Justin is by no means certain).
[2] Tatian, *Orat. ad Graec.* 12-13.

neither mortal nor immortal, but only capable of either destiny. It is only as the syzygy or link between God and man is restored that immortality is restored to man. S. Theophilus virtually repeats the point of S. Justin. If God had made man immortal He would have made man God; if, however, He had made him mortal, He would have made him subject to decay, and therefore appeared to be the cause of man's death. Man was, however, susceptible to either destiny.[1] Athenagoras, however, maintained without equivocation the natural immortality of the human spirit.[2]

Although this doctrine of the character and content of immortality and incorruptibility is thoroughly metaphysical, a more spiritual note is introduced in the notion of its restoration to mankind through union with God. S. Justin clearly states that it is through participation in the *Logos* that mankind receives this gift from God. The just will become impassible and immortal like God and will, in the language of the Psalter,[3] be deemed worthy to be called sons of God and even gods themselves.[4] S. Theophilus speaks of primal man as God by assumption, capable of rising to heaven and possessing Eternity;[5] Tatian of the close link between God and man, the syzygy between the Divine Spirit and the soul of man or the syzygy according to God.[6] Such passages suggest that the mystical element in the doctrine of Redemption is beginning to make itself

---

[1] Theophilus, *Ad Aut.* ii. 27.   [2] Athenagoras, *De Res.* 16.
[3] Ps. lxxxii. 6.   [4] Justin, *Dial.* 124.
[5] Theophilus, *Ad Aut.* 11, 24, θεὰς ἀναδειχθείς.
[6] Tatian, *Orat.* 13.

felt though it has hardly yet begun to take control of the situation.

In comparison with these two dimensions, the element of eschatology in the Apologists can hardly be said to count. The End is not yet. Man is not yet all that he will become in the fulness of the dispensation of God; but it is rather in the metaphysical and the mystical elements of their thought that the real contribution of the Apologists to the doctrine of Redemption must be sought.

A similar background is found in the writings of the great Alexandrine Fathers, Clement and Origen. In philosophy a thoroughgoing Greek, Clement blends his Christian principles somewhat uneasily with his philosophical presuppositions. His Christian Gnostic, for example, has the twin attributes of impassibility and love. The former attribute comes straight from the Greek ideal of the sage, the latter from the Hebrew and Christian goal of the saint. Without asking too closely at this juncture how far they may be compatible, we may readily see that both lines of development might in their different ways contribute to a doctrine of the redeemed Christian as in the way towards deification. Indeed, Clement is the first Father actually to use the term of the *Logos* deifying man by His teaching.[1] The Christian Gnostic is even daringly described as God walking about in the flesh.[2] Here, although the pressure of Greek

---

[1] Clement Alex. *Protrept.* xi. 114; *Strom.* vi. 15, 125.
[2] ibid., vii. 16, 101, ἐν σαρκὶ περιπατῶν θεός.

metaphysics is clear enough, Christian Mysticism is beginning to take control.

The process is carried even further by Origen. Here again the formal pattern of the doctrine of Deification is Greek, but the content is supplied by Christian Mysticism. In these days when the Mysticism of Origen is being increasingly and rightly emphasized, such a combination can give rise to little surprise. Deification is attained through the contemplation of Divine things; indeed, that deification is contemplation is the burden of a passage in the Commentary on S. John.[1] The *Logos* is the archetype of all those who have been deified by a participation through Him in the deity of God Himself, the archetype of the gods who are formed after the likeness of the true God.[2] Origen thinks almost of a hierarchy of Being formed by God Himself, the *Logos* of God and those who through the *Logos* of God have begun to receive their deification through the *Logos*. For such a deification of man to be possible there must still remain after the Fall a certain natural affinity between God and Man. This is expressed by Origen in two ways. In his more Biblical moments he recurs to the distinction between Image and Similitude previously used by S. Irenaeus[3] and based, of course, on the first chapter of Genesis.[4] But he also offers a philosophical interpretation which, if pressed hard, would raise theological problems of no mean order. The *Noûs* in man

---

[1] Origen, *Comm. in Jn.* xxxii. 27 (Preuschen, p. 472), ἐν οἷς θεωρει θεοποιεῖται.
[2] ibid., ii. 2.
[3] F. H. Lawson, *Biblical Theology of S. Irenaeus*, pp. 209–11; J. Gross, *La Divinisation du chrétien d'après les pères grecs*, pp. 145–9.
[4] Gen. i. 26.

has a certain natural affinity to the *Logos* Himself. We are reminded of the problems which beset the interpretation of some passages in the Apologists, in which it is almost impossible to decide whether the word πνεῦμα means the human spirit or the Spirit of God.[1] It is, perhaps, surprising to find that the theory of a Pre-Natal Fall, which is one of the most disputable parts of the system of Origen, seems to have played little or no part in this side of his teaching.

By the time of Origen, three points have become clear.

(i) The terminology of Deification has passed firmly and finally into the Christian tradition. An early feeling towards the idea is possibly contained in the *Similitudes of Hermas*[2] without any tendency to extend to Christians what he may have held with regard to their Lord. The hesitations of S. Irenaeus (although he finds no difficulty about the substance of the idea itself) have been replaced by an untrammelled use of the term as the expression of a mystical experience which makes man all that he is capable of becoming through his life in the Grace of God. Jules Gross[3] is completely justified (apart possibly from an over-emphasis on the Clementine characteristic idea of *Gnosis* in this connexion) in asserting of Origen: 'For him the deification of the noblest past of the human being sketched even in this life through *Gnosis*, fully realized hereafter through the Vision of God, this is

---

[1] G. Verbeke, *L'évolution de la doctrine du Pneuma*, pp. 410–29.
[2] Hermas, *Sim.* v. 6–7. (It is only fair to state that this interpretation has been strongly disputed.)
[3] Gross, op. cit., p. 184.

for Origen the goal of the salvation offered through Christianity.'

(ii) The Christological basis of this type of doctrine of Redemption is radically different from that which we have seen heretofore in the eschatological phrasing of the tradition. The Apologists insist upon the redemptive action of the *Logos* quite independently of the Incarnation. If God is the source of all good life, the *Logos* is the Lord of all good men, whether Jew or pagan. Redemption through the Incarnation differs only in degree from that received outside the Incarnation. For Clement the action of the *Logos Paidagogos* is the deciding fact, and the goal of redemption carries him beyond the incarnate life itself. While Origen is too much a man of the Church and the Bible to identify himself wholly with every element in the teaching of Clement, the goal of redemption carries the Christian into regions very different from those of the Incarnation itself. The Adam-Christ parallelism, central to the answer given by S. Irenaeus to the question, *Cur Deus Homo?* begins to be replaced by one in which man, grasping as it were the hand of the *Logos* Incarnate passes with Him beyond the spatio-temporal conditioning of the Incarnation into a world order in which the *Logos* moves as of right and the Christian by virtue of his progressive deification through the *Logos*. In this realm it might be said that the *Logos* was born free, but that man obtained this freedom at a great price.

(iii) We are here at the beginning of those traditions in devotion which ultimately went hand in hand with the rise of Eutychianism and the Monophysite tradition. If the prayer of S. Irenaeus might be described as: 'Make us, we beseech Thee, living men,' that of the tradition of deification goes back to 2 Peter: 'That we may become partakers of the Divine Nature.' This devotional attitude had a corresponding repercussion in the sphere of Christology. If the aim of the Christian is virtually to cease to be 'human, all too human,' it would be a natural corollary in Christology to regard the humanity of our Lord as problem rather than datum. If Christians were seeking through the Grace of God to become *primo quidem homines, tunc demum Dii*[1] then naturally the *homo* aspect of the *Cur Deus Homo?* was soon to become a scandal to be undervalued and over-ridden as soon as possible.

We are here at the watershed between the metaphysical and the mystical traditions. It may, perhaps, even be held that with Origen we have already crossed it. If, however, the metaphysical is still in control with Clement, it has not yet been completely synthesized with the mystical in the writings of Origen, and we shall restrict the term 'mystical' to the later syntheses of S. Athanasius and S. Gregory of Nyssa. The hesitations which must beset any treatment at this point will come as no surprise to those who have seen how closely Platonism and mysticism agree together. This is not merely true of the later Neoplatonism dominant at this period, with Plotinus the 'straight' philosophic mystic and Iamblichus in whom philosophy has been put at the disposal of religious

[1] Irenaeus, *Adv. Haer. Omn.* iv. 63, 3 (Harvey ii, p. 297).

syncretism, but even of Plato himself. Many of his fundamental positions in philosophy are the product rather of mystical intuition than of philosophical argument.

Before, however, passing to the synthesis of the metaphysical and the mystical attempted by the Fourth Century Fathers, we must turn aside to examine two Fathers, S. Hippolytus and S. Methodius, who offer a curious provisional blending of earlier and later ideas.

(a) S. Hippolytus.[1] The chief passage for the doctrine of deification occurs in the closing chapters of the Philosophumena. The background is clearly metaphysical, though in the appeal with which the passage closes there is certain advance to the mystical. Man, the key to the Universe, is not a failure on the part of God to produce a God or an angel. If God had wished to produce a God, He certainly could have done so—witness the Logos who, unlike the created Universe, is of the substance of God. Man is a being betwixt and between, who can, however, attain to deification through the action of the Logos. The appeal to pagans with which the treatise closes makes this position perfectly clear. Those who, while living on earth, have known the Heavenly King, will become the slaves of God and joint-heirs with Christ. They

[1] The discussion of Hippolytus would need considerable modification if the recent reconsideration by F. Nautin of the authorship of the Philosophumena were to be accepted. His discussion of the subject, begun in Hippolyte et Josippe and continued in Hippolyte Contra Noetum, awaits completion, and in the absence of further evidence cannot be regarded as conclusive. He has, however, raised afresh certain problems which still await a satisfactory answer.

have become God. Those who endure the sufferings which form part of the lot of humanity, receive in exchange the properties which belong to God. Those who are begotten to immortality are deified.[1] Here the metaphysical obviously passes into the mystical.

There are, however, still fugitive echoes of the thought of S. Irenaeus. The *Logos* has carried the old man. After his new formation, he passed through all the ages of life so as to become the law for every age, to establish Himself as a model for all men and to show in His Own Person that God has nothing bad. For Man is the master of himself, capable of willing or not willing, having the capacity for both within himself.[2] Here may be found traces of the physical theory of Redemption suitably diluted to fit the philosophical presuppositions of the writer. An even clearer example can be found in the *De Antichristo*: 'The *Logos* of God being without flesh is clothed with the holy flesh borrowed from the Holy Virgin, like a bridegroom in a Wedding Garment weaving it for Himself in the suffering of the Cross, so as to unite our mortal body to His power and to mingle the corruptible with the incorruptible, the weak with the strong, and to save lost humanity.'[3] The Irenaean basis of this passage is equally obvious.

(*b*) *Methodius*. Here we have an obvious blend of the physical and mystical theories of Redemption. Indeed, the Irenaean elements in his theology are completely revalued in the light of the mystical

---

[1] Hippolytus, *Philos.* x. 33–4. Note especially ὅταν θεοποιηθῇς, ἀθάνατος γεννηθεὶς and γέγονας γὰρ θεός.
[2] ibid., x. 33. [3] ibid., *De Antichristo*, 4.

tradition. Those who perceive how deeply both Origen and Methodius were impregnated with mysticism can never fail to marvel that the latter was so prominent a member of the anti-Origenistic movement. The distinction between 'image' and 'similitude' is much to the fore and the latter is defined as 'incorruptibility.' The first man possessed both the Image and the Similitude of God.[1] What he lost in the Fall was not the former, but the gift of incorruptibility.[2] Redemption is conceived in terms of the Adam-Christ parallelism, with significant variations which do not occur in the Irenaean tradition. The *Logos* does not receive any humanity, but the humanity of Adam himself. He becomes Adam created anew.[3] Similarly those who are deified become not merely Christians, but Christs.[4] We are close at least in language to the verse:

Though Christ in Bethlehem's town
A thousand times were born,
Till He be born in thee
Thy life is but forlorn.

The question which Methodius is trying to answer here, 'How can the humanity of Christ, being one, undo all the multifarious consequences of the humanity of Adam?' is one which the Irenaean answer in terms of physical redemption faces with complete success; but the form in which the answer is set is much more clearly mystical in character.

Yet the phrasing of this attempted solution by

---

[1] Methodius, *De Res.* i. 35.   [2] ibid., i. 38–9.   [3] ibid., iii. 4.
[4] ibid., *Symp.* viii. 8.

Methodius does not issue in any automatic mystification, though its goal is stated with sharp clarity. Its condition is the Imitation of Christ and demands rather than excludes our full co-operation. This does nothing to lessen the essentially mystical mould in which the thought of Methodius is cast.

(iv) The mystical element in the understanding of this tradition with regard to the Patristic Doctrine of Redemption comes, however, fully into its own with the two great fourth century syntheses of S. Athanasius and S. Gregory of Nyssa.

In that precociously youthful excursion into high theology, the *De Incarnatione*, S. Athanasius shows himself clearly to be within the tradition of Redemption by Deification already closely associated with the *Logos* Christology. 'The Word became flesh that we might be deified.'[1] Its Christological implications are used with deadly effect in his anti-Arian writings. The *Logos* who deifies cannot be of the same substance with those whom He deifies; He cannot therefore be, like us, a creature. Nor could He deify Christians if He were God by participation and not by full identity of substance.[2] That S. Athanasius at least in his earlier period regards the *Logos* rather than the Spirit as the personal medium of deification is wholly within the authentic Origenistic tradition. Indeed, in his anti-Arian writings, Romans viii. 15 is referred rather to the *Logos* than to the Spirit.[3] The argument could, however, be used with equal effect with respect to the

[1] Athanasius, *De Inc.* 54, αὐτὸς γὰρ ἐνηνθρώπησεν ἵνα ἡμεῖς θεοποιηθῖορσυ; *Epist. ad Adelph.* 4, γέγονε γὰρ ἄνθρωπος ἵνα ἡμᾶς ἐν ἑαυτῷ θεωποιήθη.
[2] ibid., *De Syn.* 51.   [3] ibid., *Orat. c. Arian.* ii. 59.

full Consubstantiality of the Holy Spirit, and becomes a commonplace both in his later letters to Serapion and still more characteristically in the Cappodocian Fathers.

But S. Athanasius is not merely a mystical theologian of the Origenistic type; he is also a Biblical theologian. As such, he was bound to turn his attention to the nature and effects of the sin of Adam. Here we find a development from earlier views. Adam, the protoplast, was not simply a Dawn Man, endowed with crude qualities and raw potentialities. He was rather the Perfect Gnostic lifted above sensible objects and every corporeal imagination, freed from every obstacle to Divine *Gnosis*, contemplating without break the Image of the Father.[1] According to the eighty-second Psalm, Adam lived like a God.[2] The sin of Adam had such devastating consequences because it was the sin of a saint. These statements occur, it is true, in early writings, but his only later modification on the point was the insistence that we are sons of God, not by nature but only by grace, though this grace was bestowed in richest measure upon unfallen humanity.[3] The Fall necessarily involved the loss of this status of filial deification. Fallen humanity has now become emptied of the *Logos*, without, however, losing the possibility of becoming re-established in the Divine Sonship or the natural gift of free-will. Two conditions are necessary if this is to be achieved, a personal act of rescue on the part of the *Logos* Himself and an act of repentance on the part of humanity.

[1] Athanasius, *c. Gent.* 2.   [2] ibid., *De Inc.* 4. 6.   [3] ibid., *Orat. c. Arian.* ii. 59.

S. Athanasius is as far from the concept of automatic divinization as any of his predecessors. This is proved by three factors. He unswervingly emphasizes the presence and importance of free-will in man; He tends to approximate deification to filiation in a manner reminiscent of S. Irenaeus himself; and he gives an increasing place to the Holy Spirit in the theology of Redemption. There are even thoughts which S. Irenaeus himself would hardly have disowned: the distinction between Image and Similitude, the equation of deification and filiation, and the concept of Incarnation as a Divine Rescue. The fundamental conception of the 'double metathesis'—'that the *Logos* became what we are in order that we might become what He is'—would come as no surprise to S. Irenaeus. Had he not virtually said as much himself? But the implications of this position are worked out with greater clarity and against a more consistently mystical background. Man would have failed of his deification if the *Logos* had not been substantially one with the Father or if the *Logos* had not become flesh. The συναφή or bond of union of which S. Athanasius speaks in a famous passage is fundamental to his whole doctrine of Redemption.[1] And this is further defined as the assumption of human nature. It is just here, however, that the difficulties begin to arise. Is this humanity a single humanity or humanity as such? If the former, how can the assumption by the *Logos* of a particular humanity avail for the sins of humanity as a whole? If the latter, can any convincing signifi-

[1] ibid., ii. 70

89

cance be attached to a humanity which lacks particularity? We are here confronted with the dilemma which was to embarrass the Greek tradition of Christology for centuries, and which perhaps has not been successfully overcome even yet. The process is further explained as our becoming σύσσωμοι with the *Logos*.[1] In short, then, S. Athanasius starts his thinking on the subject of the doctrine of Redemption on the mystical level which he derived from his great Alexandrine predecessors and from which he never consciously retreated. There are evidences, however, of an increasing return to Biblical concepts during his later period. If so, S. Athanasius was not the last theologian to become more Biblical, the older he grew. Much of the material and some of the emphases of his later formulations of the doctrine are reminiscent of the thought of S. Irenaeus, but, unlike S. Hippolytus and Methodius, S. Athanasius never allowed these elements in his thought to affect in any considerable degree the unity of his development from start to finish. If the phrasing of the mystical tradition is from time to time modified in the light of different and earlier conceptions, its essential characteristics remain unchanged.

When we pass from S. Athanasius to S. Gregory of Nyssa, we find a greater tendency to stress the philosophical basis which he had in common with Origen and less willingness to mould his thought in terms of the Biblical data. As befits one who with S. Basil had compiled the *Philocalia*, S. Gregory is deeply under

---

[1] Athanasius, *Orat. c. Arian.* ii. 61.

the influence of the old theological master of Alexandria, and it is perhaps only the fact that the profession of too open an Origenism was becoming a dangerous matter in the fourth century that prevented a greater emphasis upon these elements in his teaching.

His general philosophical background is deeply Platonist. The Platonic conceptions of universals which he describes as general assumptions or κοιναὶ ἔννόιαι[1] is basic to his theology. Indeed, his picture of the ideal or archetypal man might have stepped immediately and without alteration from one of the later Platonic dialogues. Certainly it is difficult to believe that S. Gregory and S. Irenaeus are describing the same being. With Origen and his fate in mind, he is careful to assert that he is merely framing a hypothesis; but what he states is radically Platonist in tone and has moved far from contact with the Biblical records. There is, according to him, an ideal humanity in which exists, naturally and not as of grace, the fulness of humanity informed by the resemblance of God. Adam and Eve before the Fall were more like a couple of angels than anything which we know to be true of humanity in its fallen state. They propagated their species in an angelic and not in a human manner,[2] though apparently God, foreseeing the Fall, gave to them also the possibility of propagating not as angels but as animals. This notion of primal man has more in common with the Philonic conception of archetypal man than with the Adam of the Genesis story. Through the Fall man loses these attributes which

[1] Gregory of Nyssa, *Orat. Cat.* 5. [2] ibid., *De hom. opific.* 16–17 and 22.

make up the Similitude of God: beatitude, impassibility, incorruptibility, and all the gifts of grace which made him one with the angelic order.[1] Yet, though he suffers a sad change, he does not lose the Image of God. Like God Himself he still possesses λόγος and νοῦς.[2] (Here we are irresistibly reminded of the Apologists and those Fathers who most directly depend on them.) Free-will and intelligence do not altogether desert him.[3] The total effect of the Fall amounted to spiritual death. The Divine Similitude disappears as iron is soiled by rust.[4] The analogy is not without its significance, for it implies that a return to man's former state may yet be possible.

Even in his unfallen state, however, there remained a distinction between man and God. While, like a good Platonist, S. Gregory can describe man as the copy (μίμημα) of the Divine Nature,[5] even the full possession of the Divine Similitude left a metaphysical distinction possible between God and man. There is no identity of substance between them,[6] only a certain common endowment of qualities which deserted man after the Fall. God is by definition Uncreated; archetypal man remains essentially a created being.

A return to God could not be compassed by man on his own initiative. An act of divine rescue was necessary if this were to be in any sense possible.[7] God could, no doubt, have accomplished this by a simple fiat of the divine will without deserting His own essential impassibility (ἀπαθεία). But He chose as

---

[1] Gregory of Nyssa, *Orat. Cat.* 6–8.   [2] ibid., *De hom. opific.* 5 and 12.
[3] ibid., *Orat. Cat.* 5.   [4] ibid., *De virg.* 12.   [5] ibid., *Orat. Cat.* 21.
[6] ibid., *De anim. et res.* (P.G. xlvi. 41 C).   [7] ibid., *Orat. Cat.* 8.

more congruous with Himself the long way round of
rescue through the Incarnation of the *Logos*. Here
we are back, as with S. Athanasius, in the *Logos
Victor* strain of thinking. The *Logos* mingled with
Himself a perishable nature so that our nature should
be deified together with Him.[1] (The terminology of
mixture involved in this passage recalls the fact that
Christology is not the strong point of any of the
Cappadocians.) What He assumed was humanity in
its totality. That is typically Platonist thinking of one
piece with the conception of the ideal of primal man.
The Platonist in Gregory would not allow the obvious
objection that what is generally assumed is not
particularly redeemed to have any overriding force.
A Cappadocian who had already interpreted the οὐσία
of the Godhead as a generic quality shared by the three
hypostasis was not likely to see the limitations of this
type of thinking as applied to the Incarnation.

The physical elements in his teaching become
prominent when he considers how this redemptive
action of the *Logos Victor* is mediated to man through
the sacramental life. Baptism and Eucharist are the
appointed mean whereby the *Logos* continues His
redemptive work among men. Through Baptism (as
in the Pauline Epistles) we put on Christ—or rather
reassume the Divine Similitude; by the Eucharist,
Christ inserts Himself as a kind of healing seed into
the body of the believer. The deification of the soul is
achieved through Baptism, that of the body through

---

[1] ibid., 27. Note especially συναποθεώθη τὸ ἀνθρώπινον.

the Eucharist.[1] This sacramentalism recalls, though
with a more developed basis, the doctrine of
S. Ignatius. Redemption involves no less care than
rescue. At first sight this appears like a method of
Redemption by physical insemination, but such an
interpretation would be to take one element of the
teaching of S. Gregory apart from the whole context
of mysticism in which it is firmly set. Even the term
'mixture,' which is rightly so suspect to any exact
theologian, turns out on inspection to be one way of
expressing what we should otherwise describe as
mystical union.[2] At the apex of his thinking Plato
and Pseudo-Solomon have kissed each other, the
Church and the Academy have met together. For
S. Gregory, despite the philosophical axioms from
which he starts and the quasi-physical methodology
by which he proceeds, reaches ultimately a mystical
conclusion in the light of which the whole of his
thought must be revalued. Deification is nothing less
than a short way of saying that in Redemption the
life of the whole Trinity is made available to Christians.
More important even than the backward glance to
Origen and to a Platonistic philosophy, is the forward
look to the more developed orthodox Christian
Mysticism of the Pseudo-Dionysius.

The Greek doctrine of Redemption by deification
has an importance which it would be hard to over-
estimate in the evolution of the Patristic tradition. It is
just as significant as that which Aulén describes as

---

[1] Gregory of Nyssa, *Orat. Cat.* 33–7; *c. Eunom.* 3 (P.G. xlv. 609 A)
combined with *Orat. Cat.* 45.
[2] ibid., *In Cant. Cant.* hom. 1.

the 'classical tradition,' the *Christus Victor* theory. It is, however, even harder for a Western Christian to understand. We do not in the Christian West move easily among such kaleidoscopic forms of theological or spiritual understanding. We like our doctrinal concepts clear-cut, even at the expense of a certain shallowness. In this tradition we seek to divide what the Fathers who held it would never have dreamt of separating, perhaps hardly even of distinguishing. We are never clear whether we have to do with philosophical or with mystical realities. (Certainly for minds of a strongly Platonist cast the two are never very far apart.) But what makes this theory even harder to understand is the easy glide from the physical to the mystical. In theory no sacramentalist should find this hard to compass, but the hard fact remains that we are here faced not with two entities sacramentally imposed upon each, but still readily separable, but with one realm with two overlapping and intersecting sets of relations. We do not move at all readily in such subtle and profound nuances. Each Father in this tradition has his own difficulties in interpretation and assessment, and the field as a whole, as we have seen, confronts us with a wide spectrum of insights and significances. But throughout the whole tradition one answer to the central question of the doctrine of Redemption, *Cur Deus Homo?* is given with undivided voice: 'He became man in order that we might be deified.'

CHAPTER V

CHRIST OUR VICTIM

THE previous chapters will have shown clearly enough
that the theory which became virtually dominant in
the West from the time of S. Anselm was far from
being the only one which was held in the patristic
period. There is enough early evidence in its support,
however, to warn us against regarding it as an
invention of the age of the Schoolmen.

Harnack and others have seen in the doctrine the
form of the doctrine of Redemption which was
characteristic of the Christian West. This conclusion
is in the main true provided that two limiting factors
are borne in mind.

(i) References to this theme are not wanting in the
Eastern Fathers. Martin Werner gives a catena of
eighteen references which in his opinion belong to this
tradition, ranging from the Apostolic Fathers to the
writings of S. Athanasius.[1] There is no reason to
believe that his list is exhaustive. It is evident, however,
that this tradition is not really characteristic of the
Eastern doctrine of Redemption as a whole. Some
references on closer inspection really belong to, or are
combined with, the *Christus Victor* way of thinking.

(ii) The fact that this tradition is characteristically
Western must not be taken to imply the further

[1] M. Werner, *Die Entstehung des Christlichen Dogmas*, p. 277, n. 17.

96

corollary that no other forms of the doctrine of Redemption are to be found in Western writers. The doctrine of the Recapitulation, for example, which we saw to be closely associated with the *Christus Victor* tradition, recurs in Tertullian, whose phrasing of the parallel between Eve and the Blessed Virgin we have already seen to be more closely drawn than in S. Irenaeus.[1] S. Ambrose gives a particularly interesting list of parallels between Christ and Adam. 'Adam sprang from virgin soil, Christ from a virgin; Adam was made in the image of God, Christ was that Image; Death sprang from a Tree, Life from a Cross; both Adam and Christ were in the desert.'[2] There are even a few references to the characteristically Eastern doctrine of Deification. S. Cyprian recalls the older Irenaean phraseology: 'The Son of God suffered in order to make us sons of God.'[3] But the closest parallel is to be found in S. Augustine, who speaks directly of our Lord as made partaker of our mortality so as to make us partakers of His Divinity.[4] The statement, however, lacks any of the refinements of corresponding Eastern developments of this tradition. Filiation rather than Deification is principally in view here. In view of the rôle which S. Hilary of Poictiers took in the theological rapprochement between East

---

[1] Tertullian, *De carne Christi*, 17. '*In virginem adhuc Evam irrepserat verbum* (the tempting word of the serpent) *aedificatorium nobis mortis, in virginem aeque introducendum erat Dei Verbum extructorium vitae, ut quod per eius modi sexum abierat in perditionem, per eundem sexum erigeretur in salutem. Crediderat Eva serpenti; credidit Maria Gabrieli. Quod illa credendo deliquit, haec credendo delevit.*'

[2] Ambrose, *Comm. in Luc.* iv. 7.

[3] Cyprian, *Ep.* lviii. 6, '*Filius Dei passus est ut nos filios Dei faceret.*'

[4] Augustine, *De Trin.* iv. 1, 2–3; 2, 4. '*Factus est particeps mortalitatis nostrae; fecit nos participes divinitatis suae.*'

and West, it is not surprising to find in his writings passages which are reminiscent of the teaching of his Eastern contemporaries.[1]

The appeal which the Christ Victim theory made in the West can be easily explained on the following grounds:

(i) For the West, Christianity had the character above all of the New Cult. Terms and ideas which were derived from, or had associations with, cultus had a more ready welcome than those which aligned Christianity more definitely with either philosophy or mysticism. Aulén calls attention to the dependence of this doctrine, with its use of ideas such as 'satisfaction,' from the earliest theological times upon the Western theory and practice of penance. Tertullian,[2] for example, uses the term 'satisfaction' with regard to penance with considerable freedom before his fellow African, S. Cyprian, introduces the idea somewhat tentatively with regard to the doctrine of the Death of Christ.[3] This seems at first sight a curiously back-to-front procedure in the evolution of Christian doctrine until we recall that cultic practice played an almost precisely similar part in the doctrine of Original Sin. The Western developments of the latter doctrine depend largely upon the necessity for providing a

---

[1] Duchesne, *Histoire Ancienne de l'Eglise*, Vol. ii (edition of 1910), p. 525, calls attention to the surprising fact that there is no evidence that S. Athanasius ever personally met S. Hilary. He is never mentioned in the voluminous writings left by S. Athanasius, and even Socrates and Sozomen seem to rely on the work of Rufinus for their information about him.

[2] Tertullian, *De Pat.* 13; *De Pud.* 13; *De Cult. Fem.* 1, 1; *De Jejun.* 3, etc.

[3] Harnack (*History of Dogmas*, ii, p. 133) claims that the term '*satisfacere Deo*' first occurs in the writings of S. Cyprian. Rivière has to confess that he cannot find the reference, which Harnack does not vouchsafe. The earliest reference which I can discover is the term '*satisfactura*' in Hilary.

theological rationale for the practice of Infant Baptism, which had grown up spontaneously without doctrinal pressure.

(ii) It offered what for the West would be a welcome simplification of the *Christus Victor* theory. Aulén has well brought out the essential two-sidedness of the *Christus Victor* theory considered as an act done both by God and towards God. This is alike its most attractive and most baffling feature. By contrast, the Christ Victim theory reduces these two aspects to one, what is done by Christ as Man towards God. Such a simplification was almost imperative if the Western passion for clarity were to be served. The attraction of the Christ Victim theory lay in fact precisely in its limitations. Whatever the ultimate theological issues involved (complex enough in all conscience), its starting-point was matter-of-fact and down to earth. To the question *Cur Deus Homo?* it could return the grim, yet saving, answer, '*Mori missus.*'

(iii) The legal, transactional, and practical bent of much (though not all) Western theology has often been noted. Whether it is more than a curious accident of history that the lawyer, Tertullian, despite his lapse into heresy in mid-career, was the real driving-force in Western theology may be open to doubt. Apart from a few famous names, the really significant figures in Western Christendom were men of affairs rather than theologians proper. At any rate, such a theory of Redemption through the death of the Saving Victim had obvious attractions for the legal and practical mind of the West. The transactionalism which underlies the Western Eucharistic rite is familiar enough. The Latin Mass, by contrast with the rich associational mysticism of the Eastern rites, is clear-cut and canalized. This would be in cultus a reflexion of the same tendencies which in the theology of Redemption offered an interpretation of the Death of Christ as a transaction accomplished for us in the Person of the Redeemer.

(iv) Western Christology from Tertullian to S. Leo always offered a firm insistence upon the humanity of the Incarnate Lord. Loofs and others have noted its fundamentally dualist character. Christ is both God and Man. The positive religious valuation of the humanity was not lost to the Western Church when the *Christus Victor* theory of S. Irenaeus began to fall into abeyance. In the Western Church, Christ, our High Priest, must have something to offer and this living sacrifice is focused in His Humanity.

(v) The dominance of sacrificial thinking in the whole of Western theology and the close connexion of cultus and theology is underlined by a consideration of the Eucharistic theology of the West. Loofs, with his customary passion for tabloid descriptions of theological tendencies, has described the Western Eucharistic theology as 'sacrificial-symbolist.'[1] This compact technical term merely means that Western Eucharistic theology is characterized by two features. The Eucharist is freely described in sacrificial terms. While this is far from being unknown in the East,

[1] Article 'Abendmahl' in *Hauck-Herzog Realencyclopaedie fur protestantiche Kirche und Theologie*, Vol. i, p. 55.

it is certainly more characteristic of the West. Loofs further describes this tradition as 'symbolist,' not as implying by the term what it came to mean in Reformation times, but as asserting, without explaining away, continuance of the bread and wine in the Eucharistic Sacrifice. Just as in the doctrine of the Death of Christ the sacrificial significance of the full humanity was emphasized, so in Eucharistic theology the Western Church normally took up the Eucharist into the sacrificial circle of ideas while still insisting upon the reality of the material media. The theological structure of both doctrines is identical: this is a kind of practical Aristotelianism starting in each case from what we know, and ending with a limited though clear-cut conception of what the religious realities in each case meant. We are certainly as far as possible from either the Eastern mysticism of deification, rich though not clear, as von Hügel might have described it,[1] or the Eastern Liturgy, which tends almost to lose itself among the choirs invisible in the contemplation of the Divine Essence. Werner indeed notes this close relation between the Redemptionist and Eucharistic ideas of the Western Church, but loses its real significance by building it into his general theory that sacramental categories are really a surrogate for the earlier and more authentic categories of eschatology which they tend to replace.[2]

The doctrine of Christ our Victim has certain

[1] Von Hügel makes much use of the contrast between richness and clarity, partly as a démarche against Cartesian standards of truth, in *Eternal Life* and his other contributions to the philosophy of religion.

[2] M. Werner, *Die Entstehung des Christlichen Dogmas*, pp. 480–511.

Biblical support. Indeed, there have been periods of the Church's history in which it has been acclaimed as the only true Biblical doctrine. This is now normally regarded as a considerable overpressing of the emphasis. The term λύτρον is indeed derived from Isaiah liii, but the sacrificial background of this passage has been steadily diminishing in importance in recent exegesis. S. Paul certainly speaks of 'propitiation' and 'redemption' or 'ransom,' but the generally non-sacrificial character of his conception of the Jewish Law as a whole has not unnaturally raised in the mind of Pauline exegetes a doubt whether these terms are to be interpreted in their full significance. The reaction may have gone too far, but it is probable that the meaning attached to the term 'propitiation' by S. Paul is much diluted from what it meant, for example, in the writings of the compiler of the Priestly Code. The terms concerned appear rather as loan-words, which take their colour from the new data with which they are concerned, rather than strait-jackets which imprison rather than express the New Testament realities. There is, however, little doubt that many of the Old Testament images and terms in which the New Testament significance of the death of Christ is expressed come from a largely sacrificial *milieu*. The Epistle of the Hebrews in many of its most characteristic insights resembles somewhat closely the Western doctrine of Christ considered as Saving Victim.

While Tertullian's explanation of his doctrine of the Death of Christ does not go much further than the quotation of metaphors derived from Scripture, this tradition is already sufficiently embodied in his works. The importance of the redemptive work of Christ against the Marcionite undervaluation of His humanity comes clearly to the fore. It is significantly enough in the treatise *De Carne Christi* that the keynote of this tradition occurs,[1] while the doctrine of the Redemption of the body is guaranteed to Tertullian by the necessity for the completion of the Death of Christ by His Bodily Resurrection.[2] To deny the flesh of Christ is to overthrow the whole rationale of the salvation which He brought.

The Death of Christ does not arise logically from anything in our Lord; it must therefore be something done on our behalf as a sacrifice for sin.[3] That the Death of Christ was vicarious—some would additionally read substitutionary ideas into the passage—is stressed in a passage from the *De Pudicitia*: 'Who ever paid for the death of another by His own except the Son of God?' 'For He had come for this purpose that He Himself, free from sin and altogether holy, should die for sinners.'[4] If the tendency of Tertullian is to interpret penitence in terms of penance, it is equally characteristic that for him the meaning of Redemption should be narrowed down to remission

---

[1] Tertullian, *De Carn. Christ.* 6.

[2] ibid., *De Bapt.* 11; *Adv. Marcion.* iii. 8, '*Cum mendacium apprehenditur Christi caro, . . . nec passiones Christi fidem merebuntur. Eversum est igitur totum Dei opus.*'

[3] ibid., *Adv. Jud.* 13–14, '*Hunc oportebat pro omnibus gentibus fieri sacrificium.*' ibid., *Adv. Marcion.* iii. 7, '*Ipse etiam effectus hostia per omnia pro omnibus nobis.*'

[4] ibid., *De Pud.* 22, '*Quis alienam mortem sua solvit nisi solus Dei Filius? Ad hoc autem venerat ut ipse a delicto purus et omnino sanctus pro peccatoribus obiret.*'

of sins.¹ Already the Western doctrine of the Christ Victim is in danger of becoming theologically a *pars pro toto*.

His fellow North African, S. Cyprian, belongs to the same general trend without betraying any specially characteristic features of his own. The Death of Christ is certainly vicarious in character. Christ suffered 'for us'² or 'for our sins.'³ There is a fine summary of teaching in a passage in his sixty-third Epistle which speaks of Christ as carrying us all in carrying our sins,⁴ a theme to which he returns in another passage: 'The Son of God did not disdain to take the flesh of man, and, although He was not a sinner Himself, to carry the sins of others.'⁵

Despite all his contacts with Eastern theology, S. Hilary has an assured place within the development of this Western tradition of the doctrine of Redemption. He gets rather more closely to grips with the ideas of satisfaction and of penalty. The Death of Christ was not exactly a satisfaction, but serves the function of a satisfaction; it was, and yet was not, a penalty. Christ bore not the '*sensus poenae*,' but only the '*vis poenae*.'⁶ We are at once reminded of the theory of the '*acceptilatio*' later associated with Hugo Grotius. Both thinkers recognize the limitative character of the

---

¹ Tertullian, *De fug.* 12, '*ut redimas hominem tuum nummis quem sanguine suo redimit Christus.*'

² Cyprian, *Ep.* lviii. 6, '*pro nobis.*'   ³ ibid., *Ad Fortun*, 5, '*pro peccatis.*'

⁴ ibid., *Ep.* lxiii. 13, '*Nos omnes portabat Christus qui et peccata nostre portabat.*'

⁵ ibid., *De Bono Pat.* 6.

⁶ Hilary, *Comm. in Ps. liii.* 12, '*Officio ipsa satisfactura poenae, non tamen sensu poenae laesura patientem — Dum et poenali ministerio desaevit et virtus corporis sine sensu poenae vim poenae in se desaevientis excepit.*'

concepts which they are led to use, not wholly appropriate to the voluntary, yet vicarious action of the sinless Christ. 'Satisfaction' and 'penalty' are the nearest human analogies to this aspect of the work of Christ, which cannot be avoided in any attempt to explain the action of Christ in terms which men can understand, and which yet must be marked as not in themselves terms adequate to express the reality involved. They are analogical and not univocal statements. Christ is both Victim and Oblation. God aims at the purchase of the salvation of the whole human race by the offering of this holy and perfect victim.[1] A further passage heaps up phrases to express the same fundamental idea: 'Christ is both the propitiation and redemption for our sins and the deprecation of our iniquities.'[2] Scriptural terms and phrases predominate.

S. Ambrose offers a more theological statement of the same fundamental doctrinal insight. He stands firmly with the later Thomists against their Scotist rivals in regarding Redemption as the real purpose of the Incarnation. The preoccupation with the Death of Christ, so characteristic of most Western thinking, is already making its presence felt. He is at one with the *mori missus* of Tertullian. 'What,' he asks, 'was the cause of the Incarnation except that the flesh which had sinned should be redeemed through Him?'[3] Yet this focus in the Death of Christ of the Redemption

[1] ibid., *Comm. in Ps. liii.* 13, '*Omnem humani generis salutem oblatione sanctae huius et perfectae hostiae redempturus.*'
[2] ibid., *Comm. in Ps. cxxix.* 9, '*Ipse pro peccatis nostris et propitiatio et redemptio et deprecatio est iniquitatum nostrarum.*
[3] Ambrose, *De Sacr. Inc.* vi. 56, '*Quae erat causa incarnationis nisi ut caro quae peccaverat per se redimeretur?*'

wrought by Him does not altogether lose its contact with other aspects of His Life and Work. The Christ Who was to die in a certain way for a certain purpose is still the Christ Who was Virgin-born, wrought miracles in His public ministry, and above all rose from the dead when His Passion was completed.[1] The loss of any one of these aspects of His Incarnation would destroy the saving pattern of our Redemption through Him.

The theme of S. Ambrose here closely parallels the hymn:

> For us He was baptized and bore
> His holy fast and hungered sore;
> For us temptation sharp He knew;
> For us the Tempter overthrew.
>
> For us to wicked men betrayed,
> Scourged, mocked, in purple robe arrayed,
> For us He bore the Cross's death;
> For us at last gave up His breath.

The idea of sacrifice is well to the fore with the customary Old Testament analogies heavily laid under contribution.[2] The term 'satisfaction' is only once used expressly by S. Ambrose with reference to the Death of Christ, but this hardly does justice to the dominance of the fundamental theme of vicarious offering to God contained in his writings. 'He underwent death to give satisfaction for those who were

---

[1] Ambrose, *Comm. in Luc vi.* 10–11, '*Ipse est Christus qui natus est ex virgine, ipse est qui mirabilia fecit in populo ipse qui mortuus est pro peccatis nostris et resurrexit a mortuis, unum horum si retraxeris, retraxisti salutem tuam.*'
[2] ibid., *Comm. in Ps. xxxviii.* 25; *De Sacr. Inc.* i. 4; *De Spir. Sanct.* i. 4.

under judgement.'[1] Possibly, however, the term here means rather a quittance given to the law of death applied against the sinner than a satisfaction in the sense in which, for example, S. Anselm understood the term. The Pauline crux, 'He was made sin for us Who knew no sin'[2] is interpreted in terms of Christ our substitute. 'Christ was not turned into sin, but took up our sin.' The point is put in a more extended form in the following passage:

He condemned sin in order to nail our sins to the Cross. He was made sin for us that we might be in Him the righteousness of God. Thus the taking of our sins is the mark not of sin but of piety. By reason of this sin, the Eternal God Who spared not His own Son, but made Him to be sin for us, acquitted us.[3]

Once again 'made sin for us' is interpreted as 'taking up our sins.'

Thus S. Ambrose without making any special modifications in the basis of the theory which he had received from his predecessors in the West, strongly underlines the penal and substitutionary elements in the Doctrine of the Death of Christ. He never, however, allows his emphasis upon the transactional aspect of the Death of Christ to induce him either to regard it as a mechanical process or to separate the saving Life of Christ from His atoning Death.

[1] ibid., *De Fug.* vii. 44, '*Suscepit enim et mortem ut impleretur sententia, satisfieret judicato.*'

[2] 2 Cor. v. 21.

[3] Ambrose, *Comm. in Ps. xxxvii.* 6, '*Damnavit peccatum ut peccata nostra in sua cruce crucifigeret, factus est pro nobis ipse peccatum, ut nos essemus in ipso justitia Dei. Ergo pietatis est susceptio peccatorum ista, non criminis per hoc peccatum nos Deus aeternus absolvit qui Fillo suo non pepercit et peccatum eum fecit vix esse pro nobis.*'

While it cannot be claimed for S. Augustine that he offered any more than his predecessors in the West a full-scale treatment of the significance of the Death of Christ, he certainly summarizes all that was best in the teaching of the West, and affords an important link—here as elsewhere—between the patristic and the scholastic traditions. The purpose of the Incarnation is still bound up with sin and its remedy: 'If Man had not sinned, the Son of God would not have come.'[1] Other ways of securing man's Redemption might have been possible for God, this one was more 'congruous.'[2] To a possible objection that God might have used other methods, S. Augustine indeed agrees, but doubts whether any of these would have satisfied the objector's cavils any better. The human race, then, could not have been freed unless the Word of God had deigned to become Man.[3] Portalié, indeed, notes a double process in the Redemption of man by Christ. As the Man-God Christ appeases God in the name of humanity, as the God-Man He converts the heart of man to God. This analysis, however, appears to be somewhat over-subtle. Both processes are indeed involved, but the *metathesis idiomatum* which he suggests appears rather hard to substantiate from the writings of S. Augustine.

[1] Augustine, *Ser. clxxiv.* 2, '*Si homo non periisset. Filius hominis non venisset.*'
[2] ibid., *De Trin.* xiii. 10, 13. '*Non alium possibilem modum Deo defuisse cuius potestate cuncta aequaliter sujacent, sed sanandae nostrae miseriae convenientiorem modum alium non fuisse, nec esse oportuisse.*' Cp. '*Non poterat aliter sapientia Dei hominem liberare, nisi susciperet hominem? Poterat omnino; sed si aliter faceret, similiter vestrae stultitiae discipliceret.*'
[3] ibid., *Ser. clxxiv.* 1, '*Non liberaretur humanum genus nisi sermo Dei dignaretur esse humanus.*'

Four aspects of the redemptive work of Christ can be noted in the thought of S. Augustine:

1. *Sacrifice*. In a fine passage he speaks of the continuity of function and operation between the sacrificial rites of the Old Testament, the redemption offered in the New, and the sacramental dispensation in the Church: 'The flesh and blood of this sacrifice [of Christ] were promised before the coming of Christ through sacrificial victims, in the Passion of Christ supplied through the reality itself after the Ascension of Christ it is celebrated through the sacrament of memory.'[1] The Redemptive Act of Christ is not an isolated phenomenon without antecedent or consequent in the economy of God. It has a Before and an After as the crucial part of a single process. Since His offering is itself voluntary He can be described both as Priest and Victim.[2] His offering is vicarious and operative for remission of sins,[3] though Rivière perhaps strains too far in describing it too narrowly as an 'expiatory act.' The general sense of sacrifice is, however, clear enough.

2. *Mediator*. As the one true mediator between God and man, Christ reconciles man to God.[4] Here S. Augustine recognizes the antinomy between the wrath and the love of God. 'Is God angry with us?' he asks, 'and does He view the death of Christ with real

---

[1] ibid., *c. Faust*, xx. 21, '*Huius sacrificii caro et sanguis ante adventum Christi per victimas promittebatur; in passione Christi per ipsam veritatem reddebatur, post ascensionem Christi per sacramentum memoriae celebratur.*'

[2] ibid., *De civ. Dei*, x. 20, '*Ipse offerens, ipse et oblatio.*'

[3] ibid., *Ser. cxxxiv*. 4–5, '*Ipse est sanguis qui pro multis effusus est in remissionem peccatorum*'; *De Trin*. iv. 13, 17, '*Morte sua quippe uno verissimo sacrificio pro nobis oblato quidquid culparum est.*'

[4] ibid., *De Trin*. iv. 14, 19, '*Idem ipse unus verusque mediator.*'

pleasure? But God still loves us, for it is written "If God be for us, who can be against us?" If God were not favourable to us, would He give up His own Son on our behalf?' His explanation virtually falls back upon the familiar theme of deliverance from the devil which we have already encountered in the *Christus Victor* theory.

3. *Saviour from death.* This theme is worked out with an almost mathematical precision. The single death of Christ avails for our double death of soul and body.[1] His discussion starts from two axioms: first, that Christ Himself was innocent of sin; and secondly, that death is the penalty of sin. Death therefore has no foothold in Christ Himself, and if Christ dies, it must be on behalf of others than Himself. From the text, 'I paid them the things which I never took,' S. Augustine deduces that, while our death is the penalty for sin, that of Christ is as a victim for sin.[2] His undeserved death took place to free us from the death which our sin merited.[3] The Pauline crux is uniformly interpreted by S. Augustine as carrying or undertaking the burden of our sins.[4] The guiltless

---

[1] Augustine, *De Trin.* iv. 2, 4 and 3, 6, '*Simplum eius conquirit duplo nostro. Huic duplae morti nostrae Salvator noster impendit simplicem suam et ad faciendam utramque resuscitationem nostram in sacramento et exemplo praeposuit et proposuit unam suam, interioris hominis sacramentum, exterioris exemplum.*'

[2] ibid., *De Trin.* iv. 12, 15, '*Nos ad mortem per peculum venimus, Ille per justitiam. Et ideo cum sit mors nostra poena peccati; mors illius facta est hostia pro peccato.*'

[3] ibid., *De Trin.* iv. 13, 17, '*Mors quam propterea indebitam reddidit ut nobis debita non noceret.*' *Serm. clv.* 7, '*Ille, nisi indebitum solveret, nunquam nos a debito liberaret.*'

[4] ibid., *In Gal.* 22, '*Ex poena et maledictione primi hominis quam Dominus suscepit et peccata nostra pertulit in corpore suo super lignum.*' *Adv. Jud.* v. 6, '*Non enim ulla debita ipse habuit, sed nostra portabat.*' *En. in Ps. xxi.* 2, 3, '*Delicta nostra sua fecit ut justititiam suam nostram faceret*' (the equivalent in this tradition of the double metathesis of the deification theology).

Christ took up our punishment to pay our guilt and end our punishment.[1]

4. *Inspirer of the moral life.* It has already been pointed out in an earlier chapter that this was the theory of the Death of Christ to which S. Augustine's mind naturally turned in the period immediately after his conversion. However far this may be from the final form which his doctrine took, the moral example of the Cross was a theme to which he loved to return. S. Paul, in the passage of Philippians relating to the Kenosis, had already noted the special connexion of the Cross of Christ with the lesson of humility in the moral life of man. S. Augustine is fully alive to this implication of the Death of Christ. 'Our Lord Jesus Christ, the God-Man, is both the evidence of the Love of God towards us, and an example of humility for men.'[2] Man cannot return to God except by the path of humility.[3] 'The humility whereby God was born and led to death is the supreme medicine by which the swelling of our pride could be healed, and deep mystery by which our sin could be atoned.'[4] It is this strain in his thinking which saves him from the dangers attendant upon too rigid a transactional theory of the death of Christ.

[1] ibid., *c. Faust.* xiv. 4, '*Suscepit Christus sine reatu supplicium nostrum ut inde solveret reatum nostrum et finiret etiam supplicium nostrum.*'

[2] ibid., *De Cat. Rud.* iv. 8, '*Divinae in nos dilectionis indicium et humanae apud nos humilitatis exemplum.*'

[3] ibid., *De Fid. et Symb.* iv. 6, '*Via certa qua perveniremus ad Deum. Non enim redire potuimus nisi humilitate.*'

[4] ibid., *De Trin.* viii. 5, 7, '*Humilitatem qua natus est Deus et perductus ad mortem summum esse medicamentum quo superbiae nostrae sanaretur tumor, et altum sacramentum quo peccati vinculum solveretur.*'

H

We have been able to trace in this chapter the origin and unfolding of a further strand in the thinking of the Fathers on the subject of Redemption. We have seen good reason to maintain that it is native to the West, though not in other phrasings unknown elsewhere. As a theory it has one element of tremendous strength, which had not been present in any earlier theory which we have examined. It has a strong sense of the objective character and grounds of our Redemption. There is no danger here of a Redemption virtually limited to those who have the necessary faculty of appreciation and discrimination to respond to self-sacrifice. Nor is the Redemptive aspect of the life of Christ spread broadly and without decisive pin-point over the whole without being specially mediated by any one aspect of it. The theory has its limits, but those limits are precisely its strength. It concentrates on the significance of the Death of Christ, it phrases the significance of that death in terms of offering and sacrifice, penalty and penance. It offers a rationale of the Atonement which could not fail to be convincing so long as the adequacy of certain presuppositions was accepted. It had above all the merit of being able to state with considerable clarity what Christ had come to do, what He had achieved, and how we should respond to His achievement. Could the Western penchant for the clear, the transactional, almost the cut-and-dried, ask for more? It is not surprising that in the Western Church with certain modifications from time to time it persevered until in the last century a decisive question-mark began to be set against its principal presuppositions. Yet it cannot fail to represent one element, and that an important one, in the Church's doctrine of the Redemption wrought by her Lord.

CHAPTER VI

CONCLUSIONS

It has been pointed out in the preceding chapters that there is no single formulation of the doctrine of Redemption during the period which we have passed under review. The principal reasons for this fact have also been noted. Preoccupation with other and more clamant topics from the point of view of Christian Apologetics, the number of the related issues as well as the complexity of the doctrine itself, all contributed to the postponement of forefront doctrinal consideration until a period at which the Church had lost the habit of Catholic and Œcumenical thinking.

Yet if we have proved unable to disentangle any single theory in the patristic period which might be comparable to the Niceno-Constantinopolitan doctrine of the Trinity or the Chalcedonian formulation of Christology, it has proved possible to discover four main streams of thought which, if never synthesized into a fully integrated doctrinal formulation, nevertheless provide an important quarry from which material for the construction of such a doctrine may be drawn.

This chapter can do little more than indicate some aspects from which the material gathered may prove of use to those who seek to frame in contemporary thought-forms some doctrine of the Redemption wrought by Christ, and some of the dangers in such a task to which these doctrines call attention.

It is important to note in the first place the determining influence which a writer's general approach to the Christian religion will exercise upon his doctrine of Redemption. If, for example, Christianity is viewed primarily as a way or a code of conduct, the moral example of our Lord will probably be the key-concept employed for the understanding of Redemption. Such is at least a major part of the doctrinal conception of the Apostolic Fathers, at least in the writings which have come down to us from that period. The Apologists, concerned rather with Christianity as the new philosophy, throw their whole weight upon the concept of Redemption as Illumination; but there is otherwise little to differentiate them from the Apostolic Fathers in their analysis of the experience of Redemption.

Christianity may, however, be regarded primarily as a cult rather than as a code, and here an even more significant cross-divergence can be found between East and West than between the primarily practical teaching of the Apostolic Fathers and the predominantly speculative genius of the Apologists. For the West, cultus is interpreted chiefly as transaction. The liturgical pattern of the Christian West has this character beyond doubt. Hence it is not at all surprising to find the typical Western doctrine of the Redemption of Christ as a Saving and Atoning Victim offering His own Manhood to the Father. The emphasis upon a positive religious valuation of the humanity of the Lord in His Atoning Death will come as no surprise to those who have traced the eminently down-to-earth and common-sense attitude of the West in matters Christological. For the East, however, cultus is much less a matter of sacrificial transaction than of mystical transplantation. We do not so much achieve as experience something in our cult-actions, and this will lead to a doctrine of Redemption far less practically than mystically orientated. If the exemplarist tradition tends to express the goal of Redemption as ethical redirection, and the Western cultic tradition as sacrificial oblation, the Eastern cultic tradition expresses itself in terms of mystical transfiguration.

The Eastern tradition seems still further to subdivide into views which conceive of Redemption as rescue, and views which prefer to regard it as cure. The former, the *Christus Victor* theory, needs considerable imaginative sympathy before the mythology in which it is clothed can be adequately interpreted. Here, however, as in other fields, modern psychology has come to the aid of ancient mythology, and in the light of the pressure of world forces and of personal problems we are in a better position than we were a generation ago to discover the real meaning of what such Christian thinkers were trying to express. Redemption is here conceived primarily as 'rescue,' with special consideration given to the factors from which we are redeemed: bondage to demons and all that this implies. Clearly, however, this cannot by itself exhaust the Christian understanding of Redemption from the mystical point of view. We are not only rescued, we are also cured of the miasma of sin and the other elements of our deprivation arising from the Fall. We are not only redeemed *from* something, we are also redeemed *into* something. We are not only 'brought from darkness into light' and 'from the power of Satan into God,' we are also made 'partakers of the Divine Nature.' Redemption may start from the breaking of the power of the demons; it can only issue finally in the experience of deification.

What, then, in conclusion is the part which these four traditions which we have studied can play in modern effort at the reinterpretation of the doctrine of the Atonement?

That the Death of Christ is an example cannot at any period be too often stated. It is a permanent protest against any doctrine of the Atonement which might tend to regard Redemption as achieved by any external transaction or some device whether of quasi-physical insemination or of mystical transmutation which might save us apart from ourselves. If we cannot be saved by ourselves, it is equally clear that we cannot be saved without ourselves. No expression of Redemption can be considered Christian which belittles the moral and spiritual effects of the Redemption wrought in Christ. Even the most rigidly objective doctrine of the Cross must leave room for the *Imitatio Christi* at least as a corollary or a consequent. Whether the stress be upon the human Jesus toiling up the slopes of Calvary, or upon the Divine *Logos Paidagogos* imparting spiritual illumination to the sons of men, example and instruction must be keynotes of the meaning of the Cross of Christ.

Yet, taken by itself, the exemplarist theory of Redemption is inadequate to the fulness of the Christian facts. If it is taken as more than one element in the pattern of Christian Redemption, it sets too high a premium upon certain subjective considerations, the faculty of historical sympathy with the setting in life of the historical Jesus, the strength of the imaginations of those who are to be redeemed, the appreciation of the relative factors in the life and teaching of Jesus. These are all indeed desirable endowments, and may well make the way to Christian Redemption easier for those who have them in richest measure. To rely too deeply upon the possession of such qualities for our Redemption would be to place the emphasis not upon the act of Christ but upon our capacity to receive.

Such views need, therefore, to be supplemented by the more objective aspects of the Redemption wrought by Christ such as are strongly and continually evidenced by the Christ Victim theory. The strength of such theories lies in the truth that there is about Christian Redemption a decisive 'once-for-allness' which exists as the objective ground of our salvation. The tragedy, however, of much of the past thinking of the Church on the subject of the Atonement lies in the tendency to regard subjective and objective views, not so much as emphases upon different elements in the total Christian understanding of Redemption, but rather as mutually exclusive views which must cancel each other out. In truth, neither S. Anselm can stand without Peter Abelard, nor Peter Abelard without S. Anselm. Divine action and human response are rather complementary than contradictory elements. Yet if Redemption must proceed essentially, centrally from God, it cannot, being Christian, be understood apart from its ameliorative effect upon our lives. Either emphasis taken by itself offers a result which is not really Christian. The subjective approach lands us finally in a Pelagian meliorism; the objective approach, unless counterchecked by its opposite, raises ultimate theological issues which even its most careful and enlightened exponents have never quite succeeded in eliminating. Act and Process, Divine and Human, once-for-allness and amelioration are all essential to any doctrine which is really seeking to express the length and breadth of what God has wrought in Christ 'for us men and for our salvation.'

The *Christus Victor* theory certainly carries us further in this matter. Even its mythology contains, as we have seen, elements of value, but its significance lies beyond and outside this. It refuses, for example, to divorce the death of Christ from His life. The purpose of the Christ Who came is not only expressed as *mori missus*, it involves (and necessarily involves) the whole pattern of His Incarnate Life. His earthly Ministry is not concerned simply with the necessary preliminaries to dying; it has a deeper and more positive valuation of its own. The saving pattern of Redemption includes not merely a death but a life. All this, from the point of the weakness of the objective theory taken by itself, and in the interests of the combination of the elements of truth in both the objective and the subjective theories, is sheer gain. There is, however, another element of deep significance in the *Christus Victor* doctrine. It indicates the importance of the two dimensions of Christian Redemption. It is at once an act wrought by God on man's behalf, and an act done by Christ as Man before God. Both aspects are very clear, and both demand the existence of an Incarnate Person both human and divine for their accomplishment. The Victory achieved by God must be wrought by Him if it is to avail to those who lost, or never had, any victory of their own in the press of human existence. Yet at the same time if it is to be apprehended by man and taken over by him within the framework of a morally constituted Universe, it must also be a smiting of man's foes in man by man. *Christus Agonistes*, Christ our Champion, certainly has His part to play in the whole range of our Redemption. This two-sidedness of the Redemptive Action of God, as the Act of God on behalf of man and as the act of man in relation to God, both summed up and realized in Christ, handicaps this theory from the point of clarity of expression over against the simpler and more clear-cut concepts of the exemplarist and the transactional views taken by themselves. It possesses, however, more elements of strength than of weakness considered as a description of some of the significant elements in the Redemption which Christ brought to man.

Where it fails, however, is rather in the implicit

limitation of the end of Redemption to the recapture or securing of personal victory against demonic or ideological odds. That man needs such victory is finely and truly said. That it must be, at least for many, vicarious, His, not theirs, is again well insisted. That an act of continual appropriation on our side and of abiding comradeship as our Champion on His is also involved is not in doubt. But Redemption is, after all, not purely or even primarily a negative process. We are saved not merely from something but also into something; not only from defeat but also into life abundant. This is, perhaps, the most readily intelligible part of the doctrine of deification, although this doctrine is for the Westerner the hardest to appreciate and to grasp. Physical, metaphysical, spiritual, and mystical concepts pass before our eyes with bewildering and kaleidoscopic rapidity. We seem to be committed to a baffling, if varied, pilgrimage. No sooner do we acclimatize ourselves to one set of concepts than they turn into something completely different before our very eyes. Our Western passion for clarity is confronted by a rich and profound, though obscure, complex of realities. Even our Western sacramentalism proves rather to be the juxtaposition of contrasted, though not opposed realities. To this tradition physical and spiritual are not so much regarded as juxtaposed as interpenetrating in a manner which the West simply has no terms to express. We are unaccustomed to the rich sense of the unity of all Being in God which is the most important and characteristic assumption of this doctrine, and we turn with relief to the lesser clarities of more partial expressions of the Christian truth about Redemption.

Yet the obscurity which we find here is not the darkness of a 'night in which all cows are black,' an inspissated gloom which blots out all distinctions. It is rather the splendour of light which dazzles with excess and not with deficiency of Being. It betokens the richness of the heritage which is ours in Christ Jesus, which transcends our limited powers of definition and comprehension, and which defeats our lesser clarities.

It is, perhaps, then, in the mystical realities which this group of views embodies, that we find the truest ground against which the other traditions must be set. The *Logos Paidagogos* leading his people into an ever-increasing experience of Illumination; the Christ Victim conjoined with the Passion Mysticism of the Medieval period; the *Christus Victor* offering vicarious victory to mankind, all appear as partial significances of that truth upon which the deification theory fundamentally insists: that Redemption, essentially, centrally, consists in Transfiguration, the lifting of human life out of a setting which primarily defeats and baffles because it is set too low by the participation, through all that the Historical Christ was, and achieved, in the very life and character of the Triune God Himself.

INDEX